Congratulations!

God Bless

all you Pror 3:5-6

[signature]

The Gospels
for Graduates

The Gospels for Graduates

Brent D. Earles

 **BAKER BOOK HOUSE**
Grand Rapids, Michigan 49506

With sincere affection I dedicate this volume to

Hal and **Pat Boyd**

who have encouraged me when my cross seemed heavy to bear, prayed unceasingly for me as I carried the gospel to the needy, and ministered to my family in the daily routines of life.

And with thoughtful appreciation to their daughter

Stephanie

for willingly reading my manuscripts and giving me crucial feedback from a teenager's point of view.

Contents

Introduction

Everybody likes good news. And I've got some for you. The gospel. Yeah, that's right. The gospel is good news. *The Gospels for Graduates* is a synthesis of the Famous Four. So, hold on tight— it's showtime! Now, here's the news.

When Matthew wrote his Gospel, he had the predetermination of picturing Christ as the Messiah-King. His audience of long ago was mostly Jewish. They found kings and genealogies to be interesting. Imagine that. Mark was a run-of-the-mill Jewish boy, so he described Jesus as a humble servant. He wanted the everyday people never to forget how well Jesus related to the lower class. Luke's Gospel appears to be a repeat of the first two, but once you read beyond the title page, his unique approach takes shape: Luke saw Jesus as the perfect man, and he tried to tell people so. John's approach, of course, was totally different from the other three. He wasn't trying to be super-spiritual, but since Jesus was God in human flesh, John felt a holy urgency to write it down before man twisted the truth into lies. John's Gospel says it simply: Jesus is God.

These men didn't write only from experience and imagination. The Holy Spirit inspired them. And I don't mean "inspired" in the same sense as when a poet is struck by a romantic moonlit night. The Spirit was their fire; he burned the very words into their thoughts. The result? Each man portrayed Christ exactly as God wanted people to see him, as if God had written the four biographies himself.

Now here's one thing you can be sure of: *The Gospels for Graduates* is not divinely inspired. If anything, it's a hodgepodge collection of the four Gospels, but woven with a contemporary slant. This book is not meant to replace the biblical accounts, but only to accentuate certain of their truths. Store that in your memory banks, because while I want you to read this book and get others to read it, too, you shouldn't put it before the Famous Four. After you read this, then you certainly ought to read them, if you haven't already done so.

Another thing. This is my fourth book to graduates. I didn't play peek-a-boo in the others, and I'm not about to start doing that now. Let me put all my cards on the table before we get into chapter one: *I believe Jesus Christ is the meaning of life.* More than that, I believe he is life itself. Apart from him, life is a dull, meaningless, dead existence. People need Christ. Graduates need Christ. If I didn't believe that with all my heart, I wouldn't be writing this book. I'd cash in on the stock market, buy me a Mercedes, and move to Beverly Hills.

What am I getting at? This book is designed to present the gospel to graduates. I want to cut through any prejudices you may have about "religion" and introduce you to Jesus Christ. Fair enough? Since I've been honest about my intentions, will you be honest with yourself as you read through these chapters?

For those who have already received the gospel—the "good news"—this book makes a handy devotional guide. You can use the one-a-day approach and finish it in a month, or just study along at your own leisure. Whatever you do, get to know your Savior.

10

Chances are, if you've read any of the Bible, it was in one of the Gospels. If you're familiar with any of Christ's quotations, they were likely taken from the Gospels, and the largest concentration of miracles is contained in those biblical books. We have the Fantastic Four to thank for recording the unforgettable Beatitudes and the most-quoted passage in the Scriptures, the Lord's Prayer. And don't forget that Christmas and Easter would be hard to explain without the rich history of Matthew, Mark, Luke, and John. Those guys were great. And, just think, we don't even know their last names!

This overview of the gospel message is handcrafted just for you. Its Scriptures come directly from the four Gospels and so do its truths. This is my special interpretation. Although it hardly compares with the originals, it does have one unique trait: it's written with you in mind. Matthew's Gospel was for a floundering Hebrew nation that craved a political Messiah; Mark's was for the forlorn masses who longed for hope; Luke's was for a sinful world that stood in awe of the God-man's holiness; and John's was for the fools who would question who Jesus was after he returned to heaven. Brent's "good news" is for graduates. Sure, it's a limited market, but you're the people who will lead tomorrow's world. What better group to write for?

So sit back and prepare for a little time travel. You're going to visit Bethlehem, Nazareth, and Galilee. You're going to confront demons and walk through the wilderness where Jesus wrestled with Satan. You're going to frown with the disciples when Jesus puts one of his tough sayings on the chalkboard at the Mount of Olives and cry with them when the Roman spikes rip through his hands. You will even watch Judas run out into the night to betray Jesus and then see him fall into eternity when the rope snaps at his suicidal hanging. As you sit with Mary at Jesus' feet, for a moment it will seem as if he's really standing there and you hear his voice. And then you'll be a graduate—of the University of Peace.

1 | Birth

Family Ties

*While they were there, the time came for the baby to be born,
and she gave birth to her firstborn, a son. She wrapped him
in cloths and placed him in a manger, because there was no
room for them in the inn (Luke 2:6–7).*

The Baron de Montesquieu once said, "A man should be
mourned at his birth, not at his death." A gloomy sort of fellow,
wasn't he? Imagine mourning someone at his birth. The doctor and
nurses would file into the delivery room wearing black, while
funeral-parlor music moaned in the background. Then, the about-
to-deliver mother would be wheeled in, draped in a black sheet. She
and her husband would be holding hands and weeping. Of course,
large sprays of flowers would line the room. Finally, the doctor

would stand and dolefully read a few Scripture verses about birth and life. The room would be heavy with sorrow. At last, with the final push, the baby would be born. The doctor would smack the kid's bottom, and everyone would join the infant in a chorus of wailing. To end the heartbreaking ceremony, a soloist would stand and sing a tearful medley of lullabyes.

A ridiculous scene—but I get the old baron's point. Life is hard, and this world system cruel: Little babies don't know what they're getting themselves into. True, but being born is much more preferable than staying inside the womb for several years until the coast is clear. This mourning-people-at-their-birth idea is a bad attitude toward life. I think someone needs to chat with the baron and tell him to lighten up. The worst of births and humblest of lives can affect humanity with the greatest hope.

Jesus is the perfect example. Being born in an odorous stable is not what you'd call your ideal situation. Sanitation was at a premium that night. Don't get me wrong. It *was* a hallowed birth, but the surroundings weren't exactly convenient. Poor Joseph probably had to elbow indiscreet cows to keep them from staring. For some reason, I've never pictured the nativity scene like Christmas cards do, with the stable bathed in starry beams and the manger throbbing with a golden glow. I'm sure Jesus delighted God and Mary and Joseph with his fair share of cuddly-coos, but if the stable had been such a glittering stage, everybody and his brother would have been there. The whole night would have turned into a gala spectacular, and Bethlehem would have been transformed into a three-ring circus. Jesus was born as he was meant to be—simply and silently. Angels heralded the message of Christ's birth to shepherds only to send mankind a signal: *The Shepherd of our souls was born.*

My own birth wasn't too whoopie. Not that I can personally recall the details—I was a little young at the time—but Mom was kind enough to pass along the horrible truth of how I almost became a tragedy. Her doctor must have had the Baron de Montesquieu's attitude about babies, because he rarely showed up on time for his

13

deliveries. When my time of arrival came, I wanted out, but the doc was upstairs having coffee with his daughter or something. Ever since, I've hated for people to be late. Although I finally made it, no thanks to the quack, my head was mashed into the shape of a football. I was the original Conehead.

You may not be thinking about your birth these days, but I'll guarantee you that before the tassel on your graduation cap is moved, your parents will peek into the past. Your mom will remember her labor pains as if it were only yesterday, and dad will remember the first time he held you, afraid he might accidentally break you. If you were adopted, or came into your family through some unusual circumstance, your parents will probably recollect your early days in the household. During those first moments together, the bonding began. And that's what family ties are all about.

There are two things about birth that are worth some thought for a Christian:

A noble birth isn't necessary. O, life may appear to be easier for those born into wealthy families, and such a birth has its benefits, but many of the world's greats met their destiny by rising out of poverty and facing odds that others feared to face. Paul's words to the Corinthians clearly spell out how God most uses the least:

> Brothers, think of what you were when you were called. Not many of you were wise by human standards; not many were influential; not many were of noble birth. But God chose the foolish things of the world to shame the wise; God chose the weak things of the world to shame the strong (1 Cor. 1:26–27).

There are two births. It was Jesus who introduced this revolutionary truth—the truth of the new birth. He told it to a guy named Nicodemus, a noble-born Jew. Since Nick couldn't swallow the news about being born again, he asked Jesus the puzzled question, "How can a man be born when he is old? Surely he cannot enter a second

14

time into his mother's womb to be born!" (John 3:4). Right away you can see that Nick was good at biology.

Jesus was talking about a spiritual birth, not a physical one. He was saying that a person must be born of God's Spirit to enter into God's kingdom. Nick needed a plain explanation, and Jesus gave it to him: "Flesh gives birth to flesh, but the spirit gives birth to spirit" (v. 6). And with the second birth comes eternal life. Even the Baron de Montesquieu would have to smile at that.

2 **Childlikeness**

Young at Heart

"I tell you the truth, anyone who will not receive the kingdom of God like a little child will never enter it" (Luke 18:17).

One of my favorite pastimes is to observe my children. Sounds just like a proud father, right? That's part of it, I guess, but more than that, I get a warm feeling when I behold their innocence. It shines in their eyes and radiates from their faces. Few things touch me like one of their smiles, and few things cheer me up like their laughter. But nothing tickles me like their debates—especially the theological ones.

The other night I heard Sara initiate one of those classic discussions by asking, "How do you get Jesus in your heart?" Jared, two years wiser than his four-year-old sister, answered without hesita-

16

tion, "You ask him to come into your heart, and he does." Pretty good theology. But not good enough for Sara.

"But how does he get in there? He can't fit." Good point. Jesus, a full-grown adult, would have a very difficult time squeezing into a four-year-old's heart. Provided, of course, that he were trying to do it physically and not spiritually.

Jared explained this critical doctrine with a sense of logic only children understand: "Silly, he doesn't actually come into your heart, he just *comes* into your heart."

Sara was unconvinced by Jared's unusual brand of wisdom, although she pretended to comprehend exactly what he meant. Suddenly the discussion took a wild turn. "You don't have him in *your* heart," she spouted.

"Yes I do. You don't have him in yours. That's your problem." Typical of brothers, Jared was not about to be outdone by his sister.

"I do too!" Now Sara was claiming something she didn't even understand.

"You don't either," Jared argued masterfully. "You don't even know how he gets in there."

"I do too!" Sara was sharp. "You just ask him, and he comes in."

In disbelief of a woman's strange logic, Jared threw up his arms and said, "Then why'd you ask!" Sara frowned, not piecing together her brother's reasoning, and then they both went playfully about their business as if the debate had never happened. That's children for you.

I know what Jesus was trying to get across when he said, "You must receive the kingdom like a child to enter it." Observing my own kids has taught me the key traits he had in mind. While you're definitely not a kid anymore, it would be a mistake to abandon the three essential characteristics that keep us young at heart:

1. *Believe-ability.* There is a difference between faith and blind respect, between trust and gullibility. Youngsters can be fooled into believing things that aren't true, but the other side of the coin is that they possess the remarkable virtue of accepting spiritual things

17

without much resistance. Too many of us are like the disciple Thomas, who must have been a mathematician. If he couldn't figure out every detail, he wouldn't believe it. Remember how he scoffed at Jesus' resurrection, demanding as proof to be able to poke his finger through the nail holes in the Lord's hands? Boy, did he get a surprise!

Kids are not like that. They always believe the important stuff. And once they're certain something is true, there's no way you can convince them otherwise. The little rascals are like a puppy playing tug o' war, not too strong, but tenacious as the dickens. We need a child's approach to faith, remembering what Hebrews 11:6 says, *"And without faith it is impossible to please God,* because anyone who comes to him must believe that he exists and that he rewards those who earnestly seek him" (emphasis added).

2. *Simplicity.* This doesn't necessarily mean "ordinary." America has enough blasé Christians who go about living for God in such a mechanical, routine style that even their family dog isn't impressed. Simplicity doesn't mean being plain, either. There are some who believe that all modern inventions, clothing, and conveniences are of the devil. In an effort to keep a simple existence, they strive to avoid those innovations. It provides nothing. If these plain folks prefer lanterns, fine, but I think God blessed the world when he created Thomas Edison.

Children epitomize simplicity. They speak simple words; they think simple thoughts; they play simple games; they set simple goals. And yet, they can be so profound in their simplicity. Like when Sara couldn't imagine how Jesus could fit into her heart. Do you have a hold on this trait? Or are you in the process of over-complicating your life?

3. *Innocence.* No word is more appropriate for describing kids. Oh, sure, they can be brats—unbearable in their teasing and cantankerous ways. But underneath their mischievous grins are giggles and dimples and tons of love. To them, life is composed of birthday parties, amusement parks, visits to Grandma's house, Christmas mornings that sparkle with fresh snow, and fun things like

18

football, kickball, baseball, and dollies. They know nothing about murder, or rape, or the Mafia, or communism, or why people get divorced, or why women have abortions, or any of the world's other ills. If they don't blush when they should, it's because they don't know enough to be ashamed.

God wants us to be innocent. No, I don't mean ostriches, stupid about reality. He wants us to avoid getting any of life's unalterable scars. That's not to say God doesn't forgive; he does. What I'm saying is that once a person turns on to sin's pleasures, innocence is lost for good. Forgiveness can restore a lot of destruction, but it can't wipe away the memories. Paul said it best near the end of his Letter to the Romans: ". . . I want you to be wise about what is good, and innocent about what is evil" (Rom. 16:19).

As innocent, simple, and eager to believe as a child—that's what we need to be. No, not childish, but *childlike*. Thank you, Jared and Sara. The way you teach is priceless.

③ Happiness

The Endless Summer

"Blessed are the poor in spirit, for theirs is the kingdom of heaven. Blessed are those who mourn, for they will be comforted. Blessed are the meek, for they will inherit the earth. Blessed are those who hunger and thirst for righteousness, for they will be filled. Blessed are the merciful, for they will be shown mercy. Blessed are the pure in heart, for they will see God. . . . Blessed are those who are persecuted because of righteousness, for theirs is the kingdom of heaven" (Matt. 5:3–10).

Get this: over ten million Americans suffer from emotional and mental illness. And listen! Twenty percent of us will at some time have a psychotic disturbance severe enough to be diagnosed as "insane." You're probably thinking, "I knew it! I knew it! I knew this world was filled with a bunch of crazies!" I'll agree with that—I may even be one of them. For sure, some days I'm more looney than others.

In Jesus' day, the percentages may not have been as high, but a related problem was just as prevalent. I'm talking about unhappiness. Like people today, citizens of A.D. 30 moped through days of misery and dread, searching for anything to give them gratification. Today we call that depression.

Happiness for the high-school student is summertime. School's out, the sun's hot, and the pressures of homework and curfews are off. It's like stepping from prison into pleasure. And don't graduates get the ultimate in happiness—an endless summer? When fall comes, you won't be enrolled in high school. It's over. School's out for the summer, and this time you don't have to go back. All right! Not that life's a party now. Some of you are college bound, some are headed to specialized training, and others into the job market. But no more "kid stuff." You are about to be on your own—the master of your fate. Sheer bliss. What happiness!

Jesus had a handle on happiness. In fact, his happy brand of living was so magnetic that a crowd of people followed him into the mountains one day to hear what some scholars call the most famous sermon of all time, the Sermon on the Mount. You read part of it at the top of this chapter. In those verses we have what are commonly referred to as the Beatitudes, although I go for a more punchy title, like what one man named them: The Be-Attitudes.

Over and over again, Jesus used the word *blessed* in his introduction. That's a nifty little word that means "happy." Stick that word in the place of "blessed" when you reread Matthew 5:3–10, and see if it doesn't sound weird:

Happy are the poor in spirit(?)
Happy are those who mourn(?)

Happy are the meek(?)

Happy are those who hunger and thirst for righteousness(?)

Happy are the merciful(?)

Happy are the pure in heart(?)

Happy are those who are persecuted(?)

I know what you're thinking: "Earles, you're nuts if you think Jesus had a prescription for happiness! If that's God's idea of happiness, let a poor family divide up my share between them." Okay, I'll admit that his design doesn't sparkle much on the outside, but dig underneath and see what's there:

Happiness is a relative term. In other words, what brings happiness to one person may mean absolutely nothing to the next. Different things make different people happy. Jesus ran the gamut of human emotions and conditions, explaining how people can have God's gift of happiness regardless of the suffering and misery they encounter along the way. As someone put it, "People are just about as happy as they want to be." If you want to be happy, then even mourning, meekness, and mercy can be a means to that end; but if you decide to be unhappy, not even faith, hope, and love can help. Happiness is a choice.

Happiness is more than a good feeling. As an adult you're going to experience life's roller-coaster ride. Brace yourself for a series of ups and downs such as high school never had. Forget about being perpetually happy; it doesn't happen. You may always have God's joy in your heart, but you won't always be feeling happy. However, the very circumstances that bombard your happiness may blossom into unexpected personal growth and satisfaction. And satisfaction feeds happiness. So happiness is as much a process as it is a state of mind. Philosophical stuff, huh?

Happiness is related to being blessed. It's no coincidence that the word for "blessed" in the Greek language could also be translated "happy." Having God's blessing ignites a more lasting hap-

22

piness than any human achievement can. It's truly gratifying to know you're where God wants you, doing what he wants you to do, living as he wants you to live, and preparing for what he has prepared for you. But God's blessing may at first come in the disguise of a roller-coaster low. You see, God knows that adversity makes you ready to advance. It's like the Scottish historian Thomas Carlyle is claimed to have said: "Adversity is hard on a man; but for one man who can stand prosperity, there are a hundred that will stand adversity." That is why the poor in spirit reach the kingdom; that is why the meek inherit the earth; that is why the merciful receive mercy in return; and that is why the persecuted have a special spot reserved in heaven for them. Because they stand while everybody else goes crazy.

So remember, the next time you're on the verge of losing your mind, happiness may be just around the corner. That should be some consolation.

4 Temptation
The Call of the Wild

When the devil had finished all this tempting, he left him until an opportune time (Luke 4:13).

Last Saturday, my six-year-old son, Jared, learned the bitter end of yielding to temptation. Oh, what a traumatic time it was—for both of us. He cried and I cried. He prayed and I prayed. Then we lay on the floor in his room to talk about the lessons he had learned. It was a precious moment, and I could feel our hearts being knit together as a father wishes it to be with his son. I was giving him lecture #302 in a sympathetic tone when suddenly he gave me another in his string of unforgettable quotes: "You know, Dad, if it weren't for Adam and Eve, I wouldn't be in here." How does a parent not laugh at that, or at least crack a smile?

Indeed, when Adam and Eve heard the call of the tempter, they went wild and blew it for the whole human race. Some people find it hard to comprehend that a sinful nature has been passed down to every earthling from their original parents. But Scripture is clear on this point. David said, "Surely I have been a sinner from birth, sinful from the time my mother conceived me" (Ps. 51:5). That describes us all. Thanks, Adam and Eve.

What am I getting at? Just this: Resisting temptation is a tough challenge for people who have a hungry sinful nature eager to be fed. Plus, the more you feed it, the hungrier it gets, and the stronger it gets, too. How quickly the dark side of the force takes hold of us when we follow the call of the wild!

By now you've been tempted to turn to a more pleasant chapter or even put this book down altogether. However, for some of you, this is the most crucial subject in the entire book. You may be on your way to college a long way from home, or you may be about to move into your own apartment. Your life is going to change drastically in the next six months, and the red guy with the tail and pitchfork knows it. He plans to toy with you during this time of transition as he never has before.

Some of you will make his job easy. You're so hacked off at your parents for sticking with their rules, and so sick of being treated like a kid, that you're going to get even. You're an adult now, and you want to prove it. But listen! Going hog-wild doesn't prove a thing; any pig can flop in the mud. It takes a person with mature courage to turn away from the call of the wild.

Excuse me. I'm on my soapbox again. While I'm simmering down, let me toss out a few ideas on temptation worth remembering:

Temptation comes when you least expect it. Satan isn't like a bogeyman who jumps out of a dark alley and says, "Boo!" Neither is temptation as certain to give us a fright as walking alone in a secluded cemetery on a dreary night. We know bogeymen and dark cemeteries are going to spook us, and we usually equate scary experiences with the devil. Therefore, we conclude that anytime Mr.

Evil is hanging around, we'll have an eerie feeling. Not always true. Although temptation can come upon us as suddenly as an axe murder in a Halloween movie, it rarely comes with the same kind of suspense. In fact, we can yield to a temptation without even realizing we've been tempted.

You see, the majority of people think of temptation as something that relates to illicit sex, or stealing, or killing, or something really awful. To be sure, those things have to do with temptation. But that's hardly the scope of it. How about the temptation to lie—to hold a grudge—to date a non-believer—to skip a week of classes—to gossip? Temptation comes in so many shapes and sizes that we can never be sure when one is going to pop out of the shadows. But mark this with your highlighter pen: *Not knowing when to expect temptation doesn't mean we can't be ready for it.* Set your guard, and keep it up.

Temptation almost always looks attractive. Nobody has described temptation as well as James, who wrote: ". . . each one is tempted when, by his own evil desire, he is dragged away and enticed" (James 1:14). The big word there is "enticed." When something is enticing, it looks good. Sometimes foods are tempting because they look so delicious. On the other hand, some foods will never be tempting to me. Like raw fish. As far as I'm concerned, the Japanese can keep their sushi. Most temptations, though, look a lot better than raw fish. Take beer commercials, for instance. Do they ever show some poor guy's brains splattered all over the windshield because of a drunken accident? Do they show an alcoholic freaking out with the DT's in a dry-out ward? No, they flash lights and tell jokes and depict everybody as beautiful and happy. After all, who's tempted by ugly, degrading, sickening, sad stuff? Nobody who has sense. But, in this case, beauty is very definitely only skin deep.

Temptation can be avoided. Flip to 1 Corinthians 10:13 in your Bible. Important words. I'm not going to quote them here, because I think it would be good for you to dig into God's Word for yourself on this point. This verse puts the clamps on blame shifting. When we sin, it isn't because the temptation is too overwhelming; it isn't because we're the only ones being tempted in such a way; and it isn't because the temptation is inescapable. We sin because we choose to, and that's the name of that tune. Pinning it on Adam and Eve doesn't change a thing. Isn't that right, Jared?

5 Demonism

Nightmare on Gadara Street

Then Jesus asked him, "What is your name?"
"My name is Legion," he replied, "for we are many"
(Mark 5:9).

In a minute I'm going to introduce you to an actual maniac. You can hardly wait, right? Before we get to the maniac, let me say a bad word for demonism. The occult is highly overrated and gets far too much media attention. Our society must be under some kind of hypnotic spell to be so mystified and awed by horoscopes, tarot cards, fortune-tellers, witchcraft, palm readers, and black magic. Harmless as some of these things may seem, they certainly are not of God. At the least, they are man's attempts to predict happenings within his own world. Beyond that, they are Satan's playthings designed to give man a supernatural look into the future—a distorted, self-interested look.

There, that takes care of the stuff you expected me to say in this chapter. Now let's get down to the serious business of recognizing demon activity. Demons are a busy crew, you know. Oftentimes they're at work when we don't even know it. We have to be brought face to face with fright before we realize that "Hey! Hell's angels are here."

When I was training for the ministry, I had a job at a clothing store to help pay for the tuition. One day, when there were no classes, I went to work early to open the store. About fifteen minutes after we opened, two young women came in. They were attractive but acted rather peculiar. Since I was the only employee there, I waited on them. They were looking for black capes with a red lining, and I thought it strange that both were dressed in identical black outfits. But if working with the public had taught me anything, it was that the world is full of weirdos.

"You gettin' ready for Halloween?" I asked.

"Are you making fun of us?" came a sudden retort. Obviously my cordial kidding wasn't taken well.

I quickly dismissed the bad tone with a polite "No" and explained that black capes weren't exactly in vogue. "Try a carnival supply store." Again my tone was sarcastic. Again it didn't set well. The two just glared at me, their eyes sharp with rage, piercing through me like jagged darts. They began to browse, so I left them and went to the cash-register island at the front of the store. Before the women left, they lingered at the counter where we had a display of costume jewelry. It didn't surprise me that they cared only for the black earrings and bracelets.

Curiosity got the best of me, so I ventured another conversation starter, "Do you two like black for any particular reason?" This wasn't good public relations, but, as I said, the mystery was too much.

No answer.

"Hey, are you serious about the capes?" I was relentless.

This awakened one of them from her anger long enough for her to spout, "Yes, we're going to a baptism tonight."

Baptism? *Who on earth wears a Count Dracula cape to a baptism,* I thought. (Boy! Wasn't I dumb?)

My puzzled frown invited a matter-of-fact comment, "We're members of Satan's church." They went on to tell me how satanic baptisms are done in animal blood, while I tried to look unsurprised. With guarded excitement, these two witches were sharing their most bizarre "faith" with me—a seminary student! When I countered with an invitation to my church, the witches fell silent.

"What's wrong?" I was holding back laughter. "Do you have something against Jesus Christ?"

Fear grabbed me for the first time in our conversation. An icy atmosphere penetrated the room, and the occultists bristled, groaning with anger. In seconds they were gone, but the evil that traveled with them lingered and sent shivers across my goose-bumped skin.

That experience has since given me an understanding of Mr. Legion. Although the maniac in this story was the ultimate in demon possession and psychopathology, we can see from his berserk, flipped-out behavior just how demons crowd into a person's life. Take notes on how Satan works, so you can be on guard:

Conscience has to go. As long as the guy on Gadara Street fought off evil and kept a pure conscience, the neighborhood exorcist could sleep easy. But once he allowed his insides to go against what was right, his nightmares began to blend with reality. Legion was there—laughing and waiting.

Hate has to come. When demonic control started, the maniac couldn't stop himself. He began to hate people so much that he hid in the town cemetery. Gruesome. All self-control was gone, and he evidently was full of self-hate, because he was hurting himself. Where there's hate, there are demons; where there's self-inflicted pain, there are demons; where there's extreme withdrawal, there is demon activity; where there's suicide, there are demons at work.

30

Rebellion has to grow. Here's something that may catch you off guard, because a little "mustang spirit" is good for a person. Just enough to make you spunky, enough to keep you progressive. But it was more than "mustang" with Legion. He broke every rule, manipulated every law, rejected every authority. "Freedom!" was his motto, but *bondage* was his life. As 1 Samuel 15:23 says, "For rebellion is like the sin of divination [witchcraft]. . . ."

These are the things that made those witches brew their pot of poison.

⑥ Deity

The Eagle Has Landed

"In the beginning was the Word, and the Word was with God, and the Word was God. He was with God in the beginning" (John 1:1–2).

God is the ultimate Superpower, not Russia or America. Take a gander at creation if you need proof. God the Creator dusted off a speck of power from his pinky and set the entire universe into order, decorated Planet Earth with landscapes and animals, and, with a single breath, breathed life into all of humanity. Not bad for a week's worth of work.

Thousands of years later, he again did the incomprehensible—he became a man. Jesus Christ was and is God! No gospel is complete without mentioning that basic truth. Yeah, there's a bunch to be said about Jesus the man: how he suffered like us; how he was tempted as we are; how he, too, grew weary and hungry. But what some people fail to latch on to is that Jesus was God-with-man. Remember the name given to him at his birth? It was to fulfill the prophecy in Isaiah:

> "The virgin will be with child and will give birth to a son, and they will call him *Immanuel*"—which means, *"God with us"* (Matt. 1:23, emphasis added).

There you have it. The True Eagle landed! And though no small step for God, it became one leap of grace for mankind.

Now when it comes to this "Jesus is God" stuff, the world is full of liars and heretics. Notice that "heretic" is pronounced like "hairy tick." No doubt showing the similarity between a false teacher and the little blood-sucking bug that hides in the hair behind a dog's ear. Heretics suck the life out of truth until the truth no longer makes sense.

To the heretic, Jesus is not God. Mind you, he comes very close, but doesn't measure up completely. For instance, the Jehovah's Witnesses say that Jesus is an itsy-bitsy god, while Jehovah is the super-duper God. (The Witnesses use the Old Testament term.) That's a cute theory, but it becomes quite messy in light of Isaiah 44:6, which says: "This is what the LORD says—Israel's king and Redeemer, the LORD Almighty: I am the first and I am the last; apart from me there is no God." According to the JW's, that sort of leaves Jesus out in the cold. But, if Jehovah is the only God, then Jesus can't even be a small-time god. Also, Revelation 1:17 makes things even stickier for these Jesus deniers. Jesus is doing the talking here, and he says, ". . . Do not be afraid. I am the First and the Last." Oops! Compare Isaiah 44:6. How about that—both Jesus and God say they're the first and the last! How can this be? You see, either Jesus is God, or else we have two firsts and two lasts. Messy, messy, messy. That's a heretic for you.

Mormons are even smoother in their refusal to acknowledge Jesus as God. As far as they're concerned, anybody can become a god if he works hard enough. This is a good deal for those who can make the climb, because they get to join Jesus in a whole family of gods. Bizarre as it may seem, Mormons believe that Jesus has a mommy and daddy god, grandpa and grandma gods, auntie and uncle gods, and brother and sister gods. Sounds like Greek mythology, doesn't it?

Philip wanted to meet Jesus' heavenly family. Check into John 14:8–9, and listen to Jesus blow to pieces the "family of gods" theory:

> Philip said, "Lord, show us the Father and that will be enough for us."
>
> Jesus answered: "Don't you know me, Philip, even after I have been among you such a long time? Anyone who has seen me has seen the Father. How can you say, 'Show us the Father'?"

Whew! What do you think of them apples? I'll tell you what JW's and Mormons think—zip! Read these passages to them or any other heretic, and watch them bore into the truth and start sucking. Stand clear, or they'll be in your ears next.

Two quick points and this chapter's over:

Jesus is, beyond question, God himself. There are scores of verses to support this truth, but none sums it up like Hebrews 1:3, which says, "The Son is the radiance of God's glory and *the exact representation* of his being, sustaining all things by his powerful word . . ." (emphasis added). What more can be said?

Because he is God, Jesus should also be Lord. That's the gist of the gospel. Jesus forgives sin and bestows everlasting life. In other words, he's our God. But is he really? I mean, have you yielded your life to him? Or do you call him "Lord" out of one side of your mouth, and then call your own shots out of the other? There is a very fine line between saying that Jesus isn't God and living like he isn't.

Think on these things.

7 Healing

Close Encounters

When the sun was setting, the people brought to Jesus all who had various kinds of sickness, and laying his hands on each one, he healed them (Luke 4:40).

Picture the scene in this verse. It's been a grueling day, and Jesus is zonked. The hot sun of Palestine has been microwaving the sand all day. People have been crowding around the Lord, crying for his help. He has preached and taught and performed miracles until it seemed the day would never end. Now, after only a short break, another crowd has gathered with wagonloads of sick people. The sun is setting, but Jesus is still busy healing needy people. Perhaps, for a moment, his body sags with weariness and he feels like he will faint. But jubilant shouts ring across the countryside as the hopeless finally have reason to hope. They have been healed. Jesus continues into the night.

How often are we like the people in the crowd? Wanting. Asking. Taking. It's easy to get into the habit of going to Jesus only when we have problems. When everything is falling into place, we're cool, we're slick. Let Jesus go his own way. Know what I mean? If things are out of control, though, we're first in line wanting to be healed. There are all sorts of healing:

The Healing of Memories. Today I talked to a young woman who is haunted by a horrible memory. Her childhood was scarred by a painful incident. As she recalled the story, tears dripped off her cheeks. Like most kids, she made a dumb boo-boo: she accidentally broke the glass in the front door of her house. That night, when her dad got home, he gave her an awful beating. Black-and-blue marks covered her legs. As the woman paused to wipe away a fresh batch of tears, she said, "The next day at school my friends saw the bruises. I was ashamed, but I could not cover them." Again sobs came. Then she was barely able to speak the last words about her experience, "I have never understood why he beat me that way." She needed a healing that only Jesus can give—a healing of memories.

Faith Healing. When we think of healing, we usually conjure up mental pictures of a crippled or blind person being touched by someone, and the ailment disappears immediately. The Bible does record such kinds of healing, but today's "healers" are, for the most part, con artists after a buck, not able to heal so much as an ingrown toenail. I realize that some of my readers put a lot of stock in this healing stuff, and I'm not about to say that people don't get healed in ways the medical experts can't explain. What I'm saying is, the healing comes about because of faith, not touch. If laying hands on sick people actually brought a cure, then we wouldn't need doctors or hospitals. By the way, I've never received an answer to the obvious question that pokes at healers: If there's a gift of touch healing, why don't the healers visit the hospitals and prove it?

In Matthew's Gospel we're told the story of a woman who gets healed of a terrible disease. Apparently she was a hemophiliac—a "bleeder." She literally chased Jesus down and touched the edge of his robe. Instantly she was healed! Jesus turned and spoke one sentence, and it holds great meaning for those who would be healed: "'Take heart, daughter,' he said, *'your faith has healed you'*" (Matt. 9:22, emphasis added). It wasn't the touch that cured her; it was the faith. So then, faith healing is another kind of healing.

The Healing of Damaged Emotions. That's the title of a book by David Seamands, and it spells out yet another type of healing. There are people who have been inwardly shattered, and it shows in their personalities. Some of them are down on themselves, and others are too up on themselves, if you get my drift. Those with damaged emotions pulsate with anger, or hate, or distrust, or fear, or despair, or humiliation. Take note, though, broken emotions can be healed, but only by Jesus. After all, he didn't call himself the Great Physician for nothing!

Spiritual Healing. Before you duck out of this chapter and get on with your business, let me hit on another theme that relates to healing. First let me remind you that there are people who put their full faith in the goofy doctrine that says, "Godly Christians don't get sick." Phooey! Equally ridiculous is the belief that Christians shouldn't consult doctors. The Good-Health Gospel, as I call it, strangles Bible verses about healing and concludes through twisted logic that sickness occurs because of sinful behavior. Therefore, forgiveness is medicine. Simply keep the sin out of your life and you'll stay fit as a fiddle. Are you thinking what I think you're thinking? Crazy, huh?

Mr. Job's case blows the Good-Health Gospel to bits, but tells us about true spiritual healing. Job was a righteous man, but God had a difficult plan for his life. Not only did the ol' chap lose houses, lands, livestock, and all his children, but he got sicker than a dog. However, none of Job's trials came because of sinfulness. Also, even though he prayed, asking for God's mercy, the trials continued. When his friends accused him of being a wicked sinner, God roared at them from heaven. What then? The lesson: *Refining is sometimes the best medicine.* In this way, odd as it sounds, an illness or injury can lead to real healing—spiritual good health. It did for Job.

Back to Jesus. Be careful not to minimize the magnitude of his miracles. When he healed people, they became absolutely well—not only physically but spiritually, too. He still does his brand of healing today, and nobody can pigeonhole his technique and prescribe how he can or can't do it. And he's sure no quack, like some of the other healers around.

8 Miracles

Do You Believe in Magic?

. . . Jesus asked him, "What do you want me to do for you?"

"Lord, I want to see," he replied.

Jesus said to him, "Receive your sight; your faith has healed you." Immediately he received his sight and followed Jesus, praising God. When all the people saw it, they also praised God (Luke 18:40–43).

An astronomer was having a conversation with a preacher who wanted him to take inventory of his spiritual condition. The astronomer was flippant and casually avoided the gospel by saying, "Preacher, my theology is simple: 'Just do good and

39

love your fellowman.'" The preacher answered, "Yes, and I have a very simple astronomy: 'Twinkle, twinkle, little star.'"

Some people also have a twinkle-twinkle-little-star mentality about miracles. Excuse me—I believe in miracles, but I don't believe in having idiot faith. "What's 'idiot faith'?" you ask. That's presupposing that God will do anything I ask without considering that he has a plan that may be different from mine. Idiot faith does more than trust God for the impossible; it takes liberties with the truth that nothing is impossible with God. True, with God all things are possible, but that doesn't mean we say, "Jump!" and he asks, "How high?" Before we end up looking stupid because we made a cocky announcement about what God would do, and then he didn't, let's get a few things straight about how God works:

God is true to his nature. ". . . God is light; in him there is no darkness at all" (1 John 1:5). In other words, since God never sins, evil things cannot come from him. He is perfect and pure, meaning he won't violate what is right. God can do anything except stop being God. How does that apply? Say a guy prays for a million dollars by sunrise. Can God do that? *Sure.* Will he? *No.* Why? That would be a miracle, wouldn't it? And doesn't God do miracles? *Yes, but he doesn't get into greed.* Get the point? When we're motivated by selfishness and trying to drag God down to our level, he won't bargain. Miracles are on his terms only. Otherwise, we would want a share of the credit.

God is true to his laws. God set this universe in a certain order. Sometimes he rises above the day-by-day laws of nature and does what man could never predict. But usually he lets this world function under the laws he first gave it. Pigs cannot fly; trees cannot talk; and dogs cannot play shortstop (sorry, Snoopy). Any of these things would be miraculous, but God doesn't work that way.

Let me put it where the rubber meets the road. I once heard of a family who lost their son in a tragic accident. Instead of proceeding with the embalming and funeral, they decided to pray for a miracle—they prayed for God to resurrect him from the dead. Several

40

days later the police had to step in and take away the badly decomposed body. You can imagine their grief, but idiot faith only quadrupled it.

God doesn't do magic shows. He's not a performer. Remember Satan's temptation of Jesus? Ol' smutty face wanted the Lord to change stones into bread, and Jesus refused to do it. However, he did once take a few loaves and fishes and feed five thousand people. What's the difference? Loaves multiplied into more loaves is a miracle; stones changed into loaves is magic if it doesn't serve God's purposes.

"Yeah," you may be thinking, "but Jesus did resurrect some people. Why didn't he resurrect those parents' boy?" All recorded resurrections were done to authenticate either God's message or God's Son, or both. He didn't do them just to make people happy. If God had resurrected the boy just because the family begged him to, then he would have to do it for everybody else, too. Otherwise he would be unfair.

Mark this down: No miracle happens without a purpose. Behind every unbelievable turn of events sings the plan of God. Nothing happens by accident, and everything has significance, whether it be great or small. If God does something that goes against the normal flow of nature, you'd better pay attention!

God is true to our free will. We're not robots or puppets. God created us with the ability to make our own choices. To be sure, for God to change some people it would take a miracle. But we use idiot faith when we practically demand that God make somebody else be what *we* think they should be. That doesn't mean we should stop praying; it just means there's more to miracles than bang-bang magic.

My kids love to watch the illusionist David Copperfield. That guy can really hold an audience spellbound. He has demonstrated such fantastic illusions as making the Statue of Liberty disappear in front of thousands and walking through the Great Wall of China. But illusions are magic, and magic is a bag of tricks. Master the tricks and you master the magic. People love to watch. They even beg for more. Magic, though, is a far cry from a miracle. Only God can do miracles.

But neither David Copperfield nor God will turn a beagle into an all-star shortstop. Not even wishing upon a star can do that.

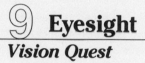# Eyesight

Vision Quest

Jesus said, "For judgment I have come into this world, so that the blind will see and those who see will become blind (John 9:39).

It was J. Oswald Sanders who said, "There are many who look, but few who see." He was, of course, talking about that rare breed of people who are daring enough to dream dreams and brave enough to make them come true. The few who see are people with a vision quest. That is, they see something others do not—something worth spending blood, sweat, and tears to get—and they set out in quest of obtaining it.

The gospel affects your ability to zoom in on life goals. Sure, you can set goals without receiving the gospel; and it is also possible that you can receive the gospel and still lapse into a dull, lifeless rut, despite God's desire to lead you to the mountaintop. Nonetheless, Jesus was right; a person's view of life changes when he says "Yes" to the gospel. His one-liner sermon had double meaning:

Blind people begin to see. If you think Jesus was talking about physically blind people, you're wrong. Naturally, when he healed a blind man, it served as an icing-on-the-cake illustration of his point. Jesus was referring, however, to the multitudes who were spiritually blind. They couldn't see the true meaning of life, nor could they find a reason to live a life driven by destiny. They were spiritually dead! Today there are people just as dead, just as blind to spiritual truths. Jesus wants to open their eyes similar to the way he opened the blind man's. For life takes on a whole new focus when we see it through the eyes of forgiveness.

Seeing people become blind. Again, Jesus was talking about more than physical eyesight. The "religious" people of Jesus' day thought they knew all there was to know about God—they could "see" everything. Actually, when it came to truth, they were so blind they couldn't find the nose on their own face. When Jesus came onto the scene, he fogged the vision of the all-seeing spiritual experts. They became blind. People lost faith in them. Suddenly those who were once blind to truth began to understand it; and those who thought the truth would die with them fell to pieces. Things are much the same today. Know-it-alls frequently lose their way or, at the very least, arrive at the end of their carefully plotted path only to find that it took them nowhere. They are so smart—they see so much—that you can't tell them anything. What blindness!

When a person trusts Jesus Christ and asks for his forgiveness, a metamorphosis begins to take place in that person's life. And 2 Corinthians 5:17 describes it well: "Therefore, if anyone is in Christ, he is a new creation; the old has gone, the new has come!" That's what inspired the songwriter John Newton to pen those famous lines:

Amazing grace—how sweet the sound—
That saved a wretch like me!
I once was lost, but now am found,
Was blind, but now I see.

Along with a new life in Christ comes new eyesight. Things that once made no sense at all suddenly come into focus, and things that once seemed eternally important dim out of sight. So what's my point? Just this: Christians should be in quest of life at its fullest. We should do as William Carey, the founding father of foreign missions, once said: "Expect great things from God, attempt great things for God." But you'll never do that with your eyes closed.

You, graduate, need a vision quest. Shoot for the unattainable, pray to the Lord of the impossible, and watch him accomplish the unbelievable in your life. Beware of the terrible fungus that opts for safety over courage, that whispers doubt instead of possibilities. Be on a vision quest throughout life. And what are the characteristics of a vision quest?

1. *God's Call.* You've got to have heart, a great sense of urgency, if you expect to become the person you are meant to be. I believe God has a call for everybody who is willing to listen, a chosen destiny for everyone who is willing to search for it, and a perfect path to get there for those who will look for the signposts. Throughout Scripture we meet people who had God's call. The Lord always had a man or a woman for the hour—Moses, Ruth, David, Nehemiah, Esther, Mary, and many others. Today he has you and me! Do you see?

One Sunday, after I had delivered the morning sermon, one of the families in my church came over for dinner. They were a sparkling young couple and full of questions. Soon the conversation turned to my call into the ministry: How did I get it? What was it? Did God talk to me? Do other people get a call to do what they do? The questions sprouted like corn in a rainstorm. "God's call," I answered, "is that voice inside of me telling me what I have to do. It's what I was born to do. If I don't follow that call, I can never be all that God wants me to be." And, yes, I believe God has a similar call for you. He may want you to be a doctor, farmer, computer programmer, or an electrician, but God has a call for you. "Well, I don't hear any call," a boy once answered his pastor. "Maybe you're not within calling distance," the pastor replied. "Get close to God and you'll get a call." If you start on a quest without a call, you'll get lost.

2. *A Worthy Cause*. Whatever you do, spend yourself on something worthwhile and spend yourself completely. President Kennedy said, "Our father told us, 'Boys, be the best at what you do. If you're going to dig ditches, be the best ditch-diggers there are.'" Remember how David was driven by the great cause of slaying Goliath? By the way, do you know what's so sad about that story? All the men in Israel's army were too chicken to stand up to that ugly wart. Thank God, David was able to see when others could not. He couldn't do much, but he did throw rocks better than the rest.

3. *Courageous Endurance*. In the Book of Hebrews, chapter eleven, we're introduced to Faith's Hall of Fame. Verses 36–38 are my favorites: "Some faced jeers and flogging, while still others were chained and put in prison. They were stoned; they were sawed in two; they were put to death by the sword. They went about in sheepskins and goatskins, destitute, persecuted and mistreated—the world was not worthy of them. . . ." Talk about endurance! Once they fixed their vision on their quest, nothing could turn them aside. Not even death.

> Open my eyes, that I may see
>   Glimpses of truth thou hast for me;
> Place in my hands the wonderful key
>   That shall unclasp and set me free.
> Silently now I wait for thee,
>   Ready, my God, thy will to see;
> Open my eyes—illumine me,
>   Spirit divine!
>
> —Clara Scott

10 Parables

Once Upon a Time

The disciples came to him and asked, "Why do you speak to the people in parables?" (Matt. 13:10).

Grandpa Thomas was a master storyteller. I loved to climb on his lap as a little boy and dig into the pockets of his bib overalls while he gave me approving looks. He had a nifty pocket watch that I'd hold to my ear between moments of admiration. But the watch was only a warm-up to Grandpa's stories. Since he was a hunter, Grandpa loved to tell about the habits and moves of animals. He even made sounds! Soon it was as if I could hear the wolves howling "down in the holler." Then Grandpa would curl the sides of his tongue and blow. A frown would crease his brow, he'd squint his eyes, and out would come the sound of the hoot owl. The whole outdoors seemed to be beside Grandpa's fireplace when I held his watch and listened to his stories.

As good as Grandpa was, nobody could paint pictures with words as well as Jesus. The Lord was an artist with words. In fact, one of the reasons why Matthew, Mark, Luke, and John (the Big Four), snap, crackle, and pop is Jesus' quotable sayings. Jesus literally wowed people. Listeners would go away from his preaching saying, "No one has ever spoken like him! He wasn't boring like that old coot we usually hear at the synagogue. Not only did I listen, but I was sorry when he finished. And his stories. What were they called? Parables? Yes, that's it—parables. They were so simple. Lots better than Rabbi Caiaphas' highfaluting blab last Saturday. You know, Jesus doesn't even sound like a school-trained preacher. I don't know, he's hard to describe. He's very different. Like nobody else. Like—God." (That's my expanded paraphrase of Mark 1:21–28.)

It's a pleasure to read Jesus' words in the four Gospels, but don't you wish you could have heard him in person just once? To have actually been there to hear one of his finely crafted parables would have been totally awesome. Which may be one reason why Jesus came then instead of now. Can you imagine? If Jesus preached nowadays, kids would want him to put on a concert, make a video, pose for a poster, sell T-shirts, and appear on MTV or "Saturday Night Live." Get what I mean? We're sort of losing our brains on how to classify truly awesome stuff. Nobody—I mean nobody!—ranks with Jesus. And his parables topped whatever charts they had in Jerusalem in A.D. 30.

"Yeah?" you may be wondering. "Well, what's a parable?" Good question. The word *parable* means "to place beside." A parable is a story placed alongside an important truth so that dummies can connect with the message instead of short-circuiting with "Duh!" The Lord's parables were more than once-upon-a-time fairy tales, though. Like nails, they drove home his point and fastened it to the hearts of the hearers. Parables were practical, down-to-earth il-

48

lustrations of dynamite spiritual lessons. They put pop into the preaching.

Here are two bites of information worth storing on your floppy disk in the file on parables:

Life is full of parables. You're just about to find that out. Incidentally, aren't you sick of people saying that to you? They mean well, don't they? But their almighty predictions of what's ahead are a lot like chocolate-chip cheesecake—the first piece is welcome, but after five slabs your stomach is in your mouth. Enough is enough. Anyway, the lessons of life are going to gradually start fitting together for you. Unless! Unless you flip your wig and completely bug out with a walk on the wild side.

A young but wise twenty-year-old woman was talking to me the other day, describing how things were starting to make some sense, finally. She topped off her conclusions with some smart words: "I can't believe how many little lessons I'm learning almost every day—things that people said I'd learn, but I didn't pay attention then. Now that they're really happening, I'm thinking, 'Wow! Somebody said it would be like this!' You know what? Through these little lessons, I'm becoming a better Christian. Every small step of growth I take as a person opens my eyes to the bigger reality of who God is." That's wise insight, Maynard. Today's tiny trials are the shoes for tomorrow's walk with God.

Life can become one big parable. For some people, parables are more like riddles. Jesus sometimes used parables to show people how confused and lost they were. Check into our Gospel passage again. Matthew 13:13 gives Jesus' answer to the question posed in verse 10: "Why speak in parables? To bring simple truth to those in search of it; and so that the intellectual giants, who have life figured out, will choke themselves to death on my simplicity" (another paraphrase from the gospel according to Earles). In a nutshell, some people gag on life because they are too stubborn to learn. They refuse to accept the fact that while life's questions are always changing, the answers are still the same. Even Jesus' parables can't help people who don't care to know the truth inside the stories.

But those who hunger for life's lessons to bubble with meaning, God hugs them onto his lap. Just like Grandpa used to do to me.

11 **Repentance**

About Face

"The time has come," he said. "The kingdom of God is near. Repent and believe the good news!" (Mark 1:15).

Unpopular word: repent. The very mention of it conjures up thoughts of a bug-eyed preacher hollering at the top of his lungs, tongue hanging out, finger pointed in an Uncle-Sam-wants-you pose. The truth is, some preachers are a study in hilarity when it comes to the way they present the "good news." They flip out behind the pulpit, so to speak. The result? Their call to repentance is more comical than convicting, more deafening than definite, more sickening than spiritual.

Not that "get tough" preaching isn't necessary; sometimes it is. I'd much rather hear the Word from a straight-shooter who tells it like it is than to have some mealy-mouthed, all-is-love kind of orator "peacemake" a crowd of people into hell. What does it profit a man, if he hears a lifetime of easy preaching and wanders out of life into a lake of fire eternally lost?

That's why Jesus hit on repentance in his sermons. He wanted to get people's attention. But throwing out a word like repentance was meant to do more than turn a few heads. The Lord was saying, "Listen, people! Until you have a change of mind and heart, you're not ready to receive the gospel—the good news. You've got to make an about-face and come to God."

One of the classic examples of repentance in the Bible is found in the Book of Jonah. The city of Nineveh—the Old Testament equivalent of Las Vegas—was number one on God's most-wanted list. Wrath was about to smother them like a California mud slide. Jonah went to tell them the rotten news after God used a bizarre swimming accident to convince him to go. (You know: the whale.)

They loved Jonah's preaching so much that the whole town repented. Check into Jonah 3:1–10 and see what odd things the people did to express to God how sorry they were for their sins. Everybody stopped eating for days, and the people dressed in sackcloth. In what? Sackcloth—graveclothes—what mummies wore to bed. They dressed like the dead. Talk about sorry!

That's not all. Even the cows and sheep got in on the act. I don't know where they got all that sackcloth, but even the animals wore it. That must have been quite a sight! People, horses, cows, dogs, cats—every living animal—wearing burial clothes! Bulletin: God saw their repentance and spared the city.

The key phrase in the story is found in verse eight: "Let everyone call urgently on God." Who do you think said those words? Jonah or some other preacher? No. The king did. Nineveh was led to humble repentance by her king. Can you imagine America turning to God in response to a decree from the President? Ha!

For national or even city-wide repentance to happen, individuals must repent. Let's dig a little deeper and really uncover some long-neglected truths about 180-degree changes:

Repentance is more than having regret. Feast your thoughts on this for a minute: "Godly sorrow brings repentance that leads to salvation and leaves no regret, but worldly sorrow brings death" (2 Cor. 7:10). "What on earth is worldly sorrow?" you may ask. Good question. It's I'm-sorry-I-got-caught sorrow; it's I-wish-I-could-take-that-back sorrow; it's I-wonder-how-long-I-am-going-to-suffer-for-my-mistake sorrow. And that is not repentance. Regrets are for "Auld Lang Syne" and New Year's resolutions. But repentance is for people who want to be right with God.

Repentance is not a clean-up act. God doesn't say, "Straighten up your life, and _then_ I will accept you." He says, "Turn from selfishness and sin, and come to me." If you wait until your life is clean to come to God, you'll never see him. Because you can't get clean enough. Only God can wash away sin. And he does it with forgiveness and with the blood of his Son, Jesus. Repentance means to turn around, to make an about-face. It's not a gradual process; it's an abrupt change of direction. Which way are you headed?

In this chapter, I've cut it sharp and laid it straight. This is serious stuff. I mean, a king actually flopped down in the dirt and told everybody else to join him! Now, if that doesn't make the morning headlines, nothing will. And all because a wild-eyed preacher named Jonah jumped on his soapbox and hollered about hellfire and damnation. That might be enough to make anybody dress up in sackcloth and ashes.

12 Pharisaism

Masters of the Universe

"You hypocrites! Isaiah was right when he prophesied about you: 'These people honor me with their lips, but their hearts are far from me. They worship me in vain; their teachings are but rules taught by men'" (Matt. 15:7–9).

Sometimes I feel sorry for the Pharisees. For centuries they have been the butt of everybody's illustrations, sort of the Rudolph the Red-Nosed Reindeer of religion. And yet, most of what's been said is true. Even Jesus wouldn't tolerate their conceited brand of faith. What can be said to defend a bunch of guys who majored in hypocrisy, rules and regulations, showboating, negativism, and criticism?

To this day, the nasty tactics of the Pharisees are infecting many churches. Their brand of legalistic mumbo-jumbo is almost as bad as the creeping crud. Once it gets a grip on a person, look out! If you're in the way, you may become a dumpster for their religious garbage. Pharisees usually do not go out of their way to be cordial. In fact, they're often rude to anyone whom they classify as spiritually inferior to themselves. You may become more than a victim; you may become a convert! And, believe me, what the world doesn't need now is more Pharisees.

Some people believe that Christianity operates under the honor system: God has the honor; the church has the system. That would be funny if it weren't so true. It's no wonder ritualistic denominations are losing hundreds of members. Who wants to be a part of a well-oiled machine that can rattle off the Apostles' Creed lickety-split? After all, isn't church supposed to be more meaningful than a bunch of highbrow mishmash?

Christianity is in danger of becoming a business instead of being the herald of Christ's gospel it was meant to be. Religion was a business to the Pharisees. They had a place for everything, and everything was neatly pigeonholed. The result? Nobody listened, and nobody really cared. And that's exactly what's happening to a lot of twentieth-century church machines. In their effort to be perfectly, professionally polished, they have lost touch with us commoners.

But there's more wrong with Pharisaism than corporate-structured ministering. Here are a few other traits that make the do-gooders hard to bear:

Rulemaking. Pharisees have a "Do's and Don'ts" list longer than your arm. They zealously attempt to keep everyone in good standing by force-feeding this code of ethics down the throats of those who don't measure up to their sanctimonious slush. The rules often take preeminence over the gospel. Oh, sure, today's Pharisees know the terminology: Only Jesus saves, God loves you, Jesus died for you, etc., etc., etc. But their bloody rules mean more to them than anything. The reason why rules are a big-ticket item has to do with how self-righteous hypocrites (as Jesus called them) look upon

55

others. They frown down their noses at them. All the while, they mark their inspection check list. What does God have to say about this? ". . . . The LORD does not look at the things man looks at. Man looks at the outward appearance, but the LORD looks at the heart" (1 Sam. 16:7).

Exclusiveness. Unless you're good enough by their nitpicking standards, you can't be in the Pharisees' group. (Not that you'd want to be.) As far as they're concerned, their way is the only way, and their beliefs are the only beliefs. To be sure, any truths clearly taught in God's Word should not be questioned. But man-made religious laws and matters of personal preference are another ball game. One of my favorite comebacks to a pack of know-it-alls occurs in the Book of Job. Three guys show up at Job's fire to console him in the grief of his devastating losses—Eliphaz, Bildad, and Zophar. Sounds like the cast of a Star Trek movie. Anyway, these "friends" rake ol' Job over the coals, displaying their vast knowledge. In his quick wit, he nailed their pharisaical attitude. Catch his sarcastic tone: "Doubtless you are the people, and wisdom will die with you. But I have a mind as well as you; I am not inferior to you . . ." (Job 12:2–3). Isn't that great? Job was saying, "It sure is an honor to sit close to you brilliant men. When you die, wisdom will die, because you're the only ones who know anything." Bingo! I bet that stuck in their craw. But that's just the way Pharisees are; if you don't hear it from them, then it isn't true.

Callousness. In Matthew 23:23, Jesus brings one of his strongest indictments against the Pharisees: "Woe to you, teachers of the law and Pharisees, you hypocrites! You give a tenth of your spices—mint, dill and cummin. But you have neglected the more important matters of the law—justice, mercy and faithfulness. You should have practiced the latter without neglecting the former." When a person becomes callous to the needs of others, he or she is well on the way to becoming a Pharisee. It can happen easily. In Jesus' day, religion had become such a super-spiritual game that the leaders were pre-occupied with perfection. They went to wild extremes, like counting

56

dill seeds in the kitchen cupboard to be sure they had given the exact requirement to God. But they were void of compassion. They talked about God's love for people, when they themselves had none. What do you think of that?

The more I think about it, the more it irks me. Maybe I don't feel so sorry for them after all.

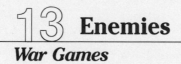 **Enemies**

War Games

"If you love those who love you, what credit is that to you? Even 'sinners' love those who love them" (Luke 6:32).

Richard Nixon probably will be forever remembered as the President who was a crook. His involvement in Watergate eventually led to his resignation from office. I was a teenager during those days, and I resented the national embarrassment he caused. To me, Richard Nixon had become Public Enemy Number One because of the damage Watergate did to our country's image and morale. But upon his departure from the Presidency, Tricky Dicky said some powerful words:

Always give your best, never get discouraged, never be petty;

always remember, others may hate you. Those who hate you don't win unless you hate them. And then you destroy yourself.

Hate is a titanic emotion. It's strong, but it sinks people. And yet, hate governs tons of us. And woe to our enemies! We want them to pay a high premium for being the dastardly dogs who cross us. Ever feel that way about any of your enemies?

I have to confess that I have. One enemy particularly stands out in my memory as the one whom I wished to see an earthquake swallow up. We called him Burr-head because he had a big, fat head with a crew cut. He was the most obnoxious person I have ever had the misfortune of knowing. Burr-head hated everybody. He wanted to fight everybody. He argued with the teachers. He was a loudmouth who always wore a bitter frown.

Once, when I was walking home from school, Burr-head ambushed me and hit me behind the ear with his fist. Oh, I wanted to kill him! But he was twice my size, and I didn't care much for fighting, so I went on home. He stood in the alley calling me names as I walked away. I never told anyone about it, because I didn't want them to think I was a chicken. It's not considered to be manly, you know, to let a goon hit you and not hit him back.

Someone has said that our lives are shaped by those who don't love us as much as by those who do. I'm pretty sure Burr-head didn't love me. And he did shape my life in a way. Really! He taught me all the wrong ways to treat an enemy:

Ignore him. That's what Mom always said to do. Moms always say that: "Ignore him, honey; he's only jealous." Right? In other words, enemies are trash that you don't have to touch. That's a far cry from Jesus' words: "But I tell you: Love your enemies and pray for those who persecute you" (Matt. 5:44). *Love* them? Now that's a new twist, isn't it? Love somebody who hates you. Sounds like a tough assignment, and you may not see immediate results. But it's a lot more productive in the long run.

Get even. It's the eye-for-an-eye, tooth-for-a-tooth technique. You

59

break my fence; I knock out your window. You steal my book; I cut a hole in your shirt. You try to take my girlfriend out for a date; I burn your house down. Revenge is the most popular method of dealing with enemies. Why? Because it is through vengeful, spiteful strategy that we can best vent our hostility and display our utter disgust with a person. Never mind how it warps you spiritually. Proverbs 25:21 prescribes a different antidote: "If your enemy is hungry, give him food to eat; if he is thirsty, give him water to drink." Another wonderful plan—be nice to somebody who is being mean to you. That should be no problem, once you get used to it.

Wish him dead. Sound strong? O, come on! Admit it. You've let your anger get carried away this far at least once. And, if not, then you have surely wished that something bad would happen to your foe. By now you must be thinking, "This Earles guy ruins everything. We can't even think bad about the Philistines who plug up our happiness." Sorry. Sometimes the truth is hard to swallow. Read what Exodus 23:4 has to say: "If you come across your enemy's ox or donkey wandering off, be sure to take it back to him." Can't you just see some Old Testament guy looking out his window, clapping his hands and saying, "Hee-hee-hee-hee!" because his enemy's $25,000 prize bull from the fair is out of his pen, wandering down the road? Listen, if you think loving your enemies is hard, and if being nice to them is even harder, then wait until you hear this: "Do not gloat when your enemy falls; when he stumbles, do not let your heart rejoice" (Prov. 24:17). Instead of having a party when something bad happens to your enemy—instead of saying, "Good enough for him! It's just what he deserved!"—help him, and let God take care of the justice.

When Richard Nixon pulled his little shenanigan, a lot of people hated him, even his former supporters. Some people still do. But what he did doesn't compare with what the people of Jerusalem did to Jesus on Golgotha. Remember what he said as the blood ran out of his hands and feet: "Father, forgive them, for they do not know what they are doing" (Luke 23:34).

And *I* had trouble with Burr-head!

14 Prejudice

Ebony and Ivory

The Samaritan woman said to him, "You are a Jew and I am a Samaritan woman. How can you ask me for a drink?" (For Jews do not associate with Samaritans.) (John 4:9).

Although I did not agree with much of Dr. Martin Luther King, Jr.'s, preaching or politics, he was unquestionably one of the greatest motivators of men who ever lived. Perhaps his most memorable words were spoken on August 28, 1963, in his speech to the civil-rights marchers in Washington, D.C. Decent people everywhere admire the courageous way he addressed racial prejudice:

I have a dream that one day on the red hills of Georgia the sons of

61

former slaves and the sons of former slave-owners will be able to sit down together at the table of brotherhood. . . .

I have a dream that my four little children will one day live in a nation where they will not be judged by the color of their skin, but by the content of their character.

Not quite six years later, Dr. King was shot down by a white man's bullet. The day after his assassination, Mrs. Jane Elliott was faced by a barrage of questions from her third-grade class in Riceville, Iowa, a dinky farm community. The ensuing experiment that she conducted was broadcast on ABC television in the spring of 1970.

Mrs. Elliott's class was equally divided between brown-eyed students and blue-eyed students. So she used this natural barrier to teach the children, who lived in an all-white community, how prejudice hurts both the bigots and those on the receiving end. The rules to her game seemed easy enough. All the students were to pretend that the blue-eyed classmates were better, cleaner, and smarter. The blue-eyed kids got all the extras: more recess, seconds at lunch, and freedom to use the drinking fountain. The brown-eyed group had to wear a paper collar around their necks to identify them as the "lower class." The results from the discrimination were horrifying:

The brown-eyed students began to mope around unhappily.

Fights between the groups broke out.

The blue-eyed students became oppressive and rude.

Some of the brown-eyed students began crying.

The whole class had the chill of animosity.

Mrs. Elliott pointed out to the children how prejudice had caused them not to like each other very much. The next day, the blue-eyed group got the surprise of their lives when the teacher announced that she had made a mistake the day before: The blue-eyed group was actually the inferior of the two. They had to wear the collars, and they had to watch the brown-eyed kids enjoy all the privileges. The results were the same; just the roles were switched.

When the playacting ended, both groups were glad. She taught them to see how dumb it was to think that one person is better than another because of eye color. "Isn't it just as ridiculous to judge people according to the color of their skin?" she asked. The children agreed and happily renewed friendships based on more valid criteria. Hopefully, the lesson will have staying power in their lives.

Prejudice is not new. Remember the verse at the top of this chapter? "For Jews do not associate with Samaritans." That's the same as saying that whites do not associate with blacks; the rich do not associate with the poor; believers do not associate with unbelievers. Jesus hurdled all boundaries of prejudice when he visited earth. He forgave the Samaritans the same as he did the Jews; he preached to and defended the poor; and he ate with sinners. Think he was trying to put across a point?

If Jews were prejudiced against Samaritans, then they were doubly prejudiced against Gentiles. In Acts 10, God sends Peter to preach to a Gentile man named Cornelius. This went over like a lead balloon with Peter, but he finally obeyed. Upon his return, the Jewish believers had a conniption fit. In Acts 11:3 they criticized him and said, "You filthy scum! You ate with Gentiles. Arrgh!" (That's an Earles paraphrase.)

Peter, of course, did his best to explain himself. He told the whole story of how God sent him to Cornelius's house. Then he capped it off with this wise statement: "So if God gave them [the Gentiles] the same gift as he gave us, who believed in the Lord Jesus Christ, who was I to think that I could oppose God!" (Acts 11:17).

Exactly! And who are we to discriminate against a person because of race, color, or social position. God loves all of us. And his gospel is offered to each of his. If he's not queasy about having a mixed bag for a family, why should we worry about our differences?

Close your eyes and imagine with me for a moment. Through an unexplainable act of God, your skin color has been changed. How would your family feel about you? How would your friends feel? How would you feel about yourself? Thought-provoking, huh?

Henry David Thoreau once said, "It is never too late to give up our prejudices." No—and it is not too late to dream, either.

15 **Discipleship**
The Right Stuff

The next day Jesus decided to leave for Galilee. Finding Philip, he said to him, "Follow me" (John 1:43).

In your opinion, what is involved in being a disciple of Jesus Christ? What is required of a person before he or she can be classified as a full-fledged disciple? Naturally, you must believe on him. Right? But what else? Must you sell flowers on street corners for the Lord? Must you pawn albums off to travelers at the city airport? Must you be clean-shaven? Must you wear three-piece suits if you're a man, and dresses or skirts if you're a woman? Must you carry the King James Version of the Bible? Must you be a Baptist, or a Methodist, or a Presbyterian? Must you go to church? Must you pray? How much money do you have to give in the offering? Can you have long hair? Can you attend movies? Can you cheer for the Los Angeles Raiders, or must you be a Dallas Cowboys fan?

Okay, so I'm exaggerating. But you'd be surprised what "flesh ornaments" different religious groups attach to the Scriptures to determine what defines a good disciple. Most of it is a bunch of cultural or regional blubber added on and labeled "Mandatory for Discipleship." In reality, it's only flab—unnecessary baggage.

For instance, in many northern and mid-western states, mixed swimming is a no-no. "What is mixed swimming?" you may be asking yourself. Well, it doesn't mean that one group swims freestyle while others swim the breaststroke, backstroke, sidestroke, or butterfly. That would be "mixed" swimming, literally. What it means is, no swimming with the opposite sex. In many places this is a touchy subject. However, Jesus never mentioned it. Since he walked on water, maybe we should assume that he was against swimming altogether. Sometimes the logic people use for setting standards of discipleship seems about that twisted.

Since Jesus set the pace for the first disciples, and since he is the Lord, maybe we should go by his standards. Good idea? I knew you'd agree.

Requirement #1: Take up your cross. Then Jesus said to his disciples, "If anyone would come after me, he must deny himself and take up his cross and follow me" (Matt. 16:24). He didn't mean that you have to lug around a huge hunk of wood to become a disciple. Aren't you relieved? Hauling a cross to work or class would be difficult to explain: "Well, uh, this is my, uh, cross. I, uh, carry it because, uh, I want to be a disciple." Yes? And if you want to be a pilot, do you carry an airplane? If you want to be a secretary, do you carry a word processor? Sure, I know that's ridiculous. But the market for martyrs is a little flooded right now, and I'd like to steer you away from it. There are plenty of down-in-the-mouth Christians, crying, "Life is hard, but I don't mind suffering for Jesus. I guess it's just the cross I have to bear." Blah! True disciples know better than to emphasize the negative aspect of suffering, although the cross *is*

66

the emblem of sacrifice. A disciple's life is one of sacrifice; he gives himself to complete obedience, in recognition of the ultimate sacrifice made by Jesus to fulfill God's will on earth.

Requirement #2: Relinquish all earthly pursuits. Move to the hills, live in a commune, and become a scuzzy hermit. Right? Wrong! Jesus is not anti-goals or down on personal achievement. His call to discipleship simply requires that all areas of life be surrendered to him. Then he blesses us and rewards us as we grow in him. All milestones become an opportunity to praise him. He was clear on this point: ". . . any of you who does not give up everything he has cannot be my disciple" (Luke 14:33). These are hard words to some people. Material gain and earthly pleasure are just more important to them. Creature comforts outweigh the Creator. Not that Jesus deprives his disciples. On the contrary: he provides abundantly for their needs. But the difference is, they know he is the Provider, while the "self-sufficient" ignorantly think they got theirs on their own. True disciples hold worldly dreams loosely.

Requirement #3: Love each other. That's supposed to come naturally for disciples. True disciples are to have a love for each other. It's a tall order, I know, but Jesus said so: "All men will know that you are my disciples if you love one another" (John 13:35). "But Jesus hadn't met some of the people in my church," you say. Amen! I'm with you. There are some unlovelies, aren't there? And yet, true disciples overlook the halitosis, body odors, and all that. They recognize that other believers belong to Jesus, too. Even if they do have a lot of growing to do. Don't we all?

Requirement #4: Bear fruit. (No wisecracks about "fruits," please.) Jesus diagrammed the fruitbearing principle on the chalkboard when he said, "This is to my Father's glory, that you bear much fruit, showing yourselves to be my disciples" (John 15:8). No fruit, no discipleship. It's that simple. True disciples have a peachy spirit and grape, grape joy. A bad pun, maybe, but true. They harvest new converts by sharing the gospel with the unsaved. What does Proverbs 11:30 say? "The fruit of the righteous is a tree of life, and he

67

who wins souls is wise." I'm afraid that some so-called disciples are actually rotten apples. They talk the talk, but they don't walk the walk. But then, this stuff isn't a cinch to put into practice.

No wonder people would rather harp about mixed swimming.

16 Servanthood

For Whom the Bell Tolls

Sitting down, Jesus called the Twelve and said, "If anyone wants to be first, he must be the very last, and the servant of all" (Mark 9:35).

Want to know something that really tightens my jaws? The political games some preachers play within their denominations in order to climb the ladder of success. I don't mean to disillusion you about the ministry, for not all church leaders fit this description. But there are more than a few fellows caught up in the you-scratch-my-back-and-I'll-scratch-yours scheme. These types are promotion-oriented instead of people-oriented. They are money grubbers instead of ministering saints. They would rather make a buck than save a soul (if they even know how souls are saved). They would rather have a big, influential congregation and be loved by everybody than risk it all by sticking with the never-changing gospel. In short, they would rather be applauded as celebrities in the limelight than be called the servants of Jesus.

Yeah, I know that's strong language. But I've been around the ministry long enough to get a belly full of these "Diotrephes" saints. "Diotre-who?" you ask. You know, the guy in 3 John "who loves to be first" (3 John 9). Better known as Mr. Church Boss. That's right, preachers aren't the only guilty ones when it comes to grandstanding for God.

There was a Diotrephes in my first church. I was fresh out of college and ready to reorganize the world. My zeal was often faster to speak than my wisdom was—what little wisdom I had. Of course, this usually didn't set well with Mr. Church Boss. I was too young to know better and handled matters like a bull in a china shop. Eventually, after learning the hard way (one of my favorite ways to learn), I caught on to the Boss's subtle ways of manipulation and control. While I loved him and tried to minister to him, I believe my ability to serve him was hampered by his greater interest in running the show.

If you have spent any time around church ministry, then you probably have witnessed a scene with a Diotrephes as self-appointed star and director. You may have seen so much of it that you're turned off by spiritual things in general. Bad experiences can do that to a person. Others of you may not have been around church very much, and maybe this is the reason why. I have often heard it said, "Who needs church if it's just a playground for hypocrites?" The accusation is sometimes correct, but the solution is not. With adulthood comes responsibility. You, graduate, must begin to shoulder the responsibility of what will happen to our churches tomorrow. If you belong to Jesus Christ, he wants you to minister in his church, to serve in his name.

"But how can I change things?" you wonder. "How can I turn the tide? How can I get people to listen to my ideas? How can I be an influence?"

Those are significant questions. Just remember: even though the questions may change, the answers are usually the same. If you stick with the fundamentals, you can have an influence. The most fundamental fundamental is servanthood. If your bell tolls for yourself alone, it's just a lot of noise, and the Diotrephes-complex will get you. But if it tolls for others, those sounds will make beautiful music. Here are some keys to being a profitable servant:

Anonymity. Behind the scenes. Little recognition. No applause. No spotlight. Just plain, silent, and secretive. The way Rufus did it. And Asyncritus. And Philologus. And Nereus. Read about them in Romans 16. There's a whole list of unknowns in that chapter. Those who serve quietly are often the most respected ones; and when they speak, even E. F. Hutton listens. If you are able to serve without an audience, then you're unselfish enough to be trusted when the audience needs leadership. Meditate on this poem about anonymous service (written, by the way, anonymously):

> The limelight sparkles, and I like it
> when they call my name;
> I think I'd like fame.
> Popularity feels good; you know
> it's hard not to pause
> when I hear applause.
> I wonder, Jesus, how high I'll go
> if I am like thee,
> where no one can see.

Willingness. Perhaps the greatest trait of true servants is their availability. They are willing to tackle any task. No job is too dirty; no toil is too tedious; no favor is too imposing. Servants want to serve. Paul, the "famous" apostle, preferred to be known as a servant rather than a saint. Hear his words and imagine them as a part of your autobiography:

So then, men ought to regard us as servants of Christ. . . . To this

71

very hour we go hungry and thirsty, we are in rags, we are brutally treated, we are homeless. We work hard with our hands. When we are cursed, we bless; when we are persecuted, we endure it; when we are slandered, we answer kindly. Up to this moment we have become the scum of the earth, the refuse of the world [1 Cor. 4:1, 11–13].

"No, thanks!" you say? I don't blame you. Don't fear! Being a servant doesn't necessarily mean you have to become a punching bag. But even if you do take a few uppercuts, you will still be willing to finish the Savior's business.

Faithfulness. This one is kin to willingness. Basically, it means you're like a Timex watch: "Takes a licking and keeps on ticking." Servants are always there when you need them. Dependability is their middle name, and thoroughness rules their game. How accurate is your you-can-count-on-me meter?

It was this brand of service that inspired John Donne to pen his famous lines in his special devotional book: "No man is an island . . . . I am involved in mankind; and therefore never send to know for whom the bell tolls; it tolls for thee."

That includes the hypocrites.

17 Intensity
Blood, Sweat, and Tears

*And being in anguish, he prayed more earnestly, and
his sweat was like drops of blood falling to the ground
(Luke 22:44).*

Switzerland is home to the majestic Swiss Alps. There is a
quaint old cemetery there in which many of the great mountain
climbers are buried. Seasoned tombstones proudly proclaim epi-
taphs appropriate to the rugged souls they describe. On one of the
stones, three words are carved beneath the name of a gutsy but
unsuccessful climber who died while trying to reach a peak long
ago. The words form the perfect epitaph: "He died climbing!"

Isn't that a great thing to have said about you, especially on your tombstone, for generations to see? What might typically be said of people today? How about:

"He died watching the Super Bowl" (man's favorite pastime).

"She died talking on the telephone" (woman's favorite pastime).

"She died shopping" (woman's second favorite pastime).

"He died reading the newspaper" (how man hides from woman).

"He died watching New Year's bowl games" (man's second favorite pastime).

"She died dieting" (woman's least-favorite pastime).

Someone once asked me how I'd like to die. Pretty morbid, huh? I don't know what possesses people to harp on death. Not that I'm afraid of it, but there isn't a whole lot I can do to control the way I croak. There are some ways I wouldn't want to go. Keep me away from fire; I don't want to exit this life as a crispy critter. Neither is drowning my idea of a smooth departure. And stabbing, gunshot wounds, and bludgeoning all sound too messy for my style.

Let's see: Would I want to die praying? Or reading my Bible? Or preaching? Or witnessing? Or writing another book for graduates? (Evidently I lived long enough to finish this one.) Answer: I couldn't care less. Actually, I'd rather not die until I'm about 110 years old, perhaps of a broken neck while playing tackle football with a bunch of teenagers.

Falling off a mountain isn't exactly a pleasant way to say good-bye. But at least our hero died climbing! He didn't die a coward; he didn't die wishing; he didn't die a lazy bum. He died climbing. Still going at it. Still brave. Still pawing and clawing to get another foot higher. To me, that's intensity. Knowing the price of failure, but pressing on with fearlessness in the face of risk.

Jesus was intense. From the time he began his ministry at the age of thirty, he carefully calculated his objectives. He got maximum return out of every day he lived. Nothing was wasted. Even the fun

74

and laughter were satisfying and meaningful. In getting the most out of his life, Jesus demonstrated how intensity brings abundance. Judas missed it, for the betrayer never knew the meaning of spending himself. In the end, he hanged himself—guilty and empty.

Scale these mountains and you will find the gratifying rewards that sit atop the peaks of intensity:

Dedication. Intensity means you eat, sleep, and drink whatever it is you are dedicated to accomplish. If you want to be a doctor, you had better start eating biology, sleeping chemistry (Note: not sleeping *in* chemistry), and drinking physiology. Otherwise, you'll be lucky to make veterinarian. Intensity is a tough, gut-wrenching commitment. Spur-of-the-moment promises are worthless and soon burn out like a dying comet. Read Proverbs 20:25: "It is a trap for a man to dedicate something rashly and only later to consider his vows." The bottom line on dedication: Get in or get out. Don't set sail with Jesus and then jump overboard.

Courage. Look, throwing your gear in with Jesus isn't an easy life. The way of the world is the lap of luxury. But with Christ comes suffering, trials, and rejection. Those who are weak of stomach should stick with baby food out of the jar. Follow the Jesus-brick road and expect God's heavenly hammer and chisel to chip away your unsightly features. Result? With each blow you become a little more like his Son. As Paul closes out First Corinthians, he emphasizes the importance of remaining courageous in the faith: "Be on your guard; stand firm in the faith; be men of courage; be strong" (1 Cor. 16:13). Without brave ambitions you will be crushed like a roach caught in a stampede.

Sacrifice. Most good athletes are considered to be intense competitors who make great sacrifices to excel in sports. Diving, racing, sliding, and straining, the athlete will pay a steep physical price in order to win. And athletes will forgo many simple pleasures that might distract their attention from the ultimate goal. The lesson is loud and clear: Unless you learn to sacrifice, you will be mediocre. Intense people give their all. Like Jesus. He prayed so intensely that

75

his sweat turned into blood. But that was his way. He never did anything halfheartedly.

How about you? Could you be dedicated, courageous, and sacrificial? Intense about life? Would you be able to die climbing? If not, you have already begun to die.

18 **Frustration**

Mission Impossible

But Martha was distracted by all the preparations that had to be made. She came to him and asked, "Lord, don't you care that my sister has left me to do the work by myself? Tell her to help me!" (Luke 10:40).

Three years ago, I began writing a book about frustration. Talk about Mission Impossible! Snag after snag has interfered with my progress. In fact, I'm still working on it, though it's just about finished. However, you would never guess how many frustrating events have come into my life and ministry during the preparation of the manuscript to be entitled *Bouncing Back: Handling the Humor and Heartache of Frustration.* So many things have happened to frustrate Jane and me in the last three years that I now feel overqualified to write on the subject. Hard to believe? Check into our "fun" experiences:

1. Upon resigning my first church, we waited ten months for God's leading into a new ministry. The cupboards were bare.
2. I had four bouts with acute bronchitis.
3. We couldn't sell our house.
4. We couldn't move, and the drive was fifty miles one way.
5. We couldn't find another house we liked.
6. My wife and five-year-old-daughter were in a car crash with a semi truck.
7. I began to get behind in my writing.
8. The dog died.
9. The cat ran away for two weeks and then came back half dead.
10. Jane got three traffic tickets in a four-month period.
11. The large church and school in my new ministry ate up my time during the transition.
12. One of our former teachers was charged with gross misconduct.
13. One of our church's most faithful men suffered a massive stroke.
14. I began to get *far* behind in my writing.
15. Several teenage girls came forward to reveal misconduct by one of the church's former youth workers.
16. We finally moved—after five long months!
17. Shortly after moving into our new home, a pipe burst and flooded the place.
18. I had a bout with kidney stones.
19. I overfertilized the lawn and killed the grass.
20. I began to forget how to write.

There you have twenty ways to lose your mind! Have I sufficiently earned your sympathy? If not your sympathy, how about your pity?

My level of frustration was soaring. I can remember coming home one afternoon (the car had broken down) and crying, just bursting out in tears. Most grown men aren't given to such outbursts, but the pressure was driving me nuts! Some of the things I want to share with you about frustration are only a nutshell of what should some-day be in print when I complete Mission Impossible.

Frustration shows our weakness. People don't like to admit weakness. Being stubborn and independent, most of us pretend to be strong, even when life has us by the throat. And yet, confessing our weakness to God is just what he wants. Self-sufficiency instead of God-sufficiency will get you out of his plan so fast that your head will spin. My deepest frustrations were caused by trying to *humanly* solve my problems. It didn't work. All I got were forehead bruises from banging my head against a brick wall. But when I finally real-ized I couldn't do it on my own, a peace settled over me. Although things didn't brighten up right away, I received something special to carry me through—grace. Paul knew what frustration was like. He had a thorn in the flesh, as he described it. Use your highlighter pen on these words: "But [the Lord] said to me, 'My grace is sufficient for you, for my power is made perfect in weakness'" (2 Cor. 12:9). Few things reveal weakness like frustration.

Frustration grows out of wrong priorities. Flip back to the title verse for a second. What was eating at Martha? She was aggra-vated that her sister, Mary, was just sitting on her hindquarters while there was much work to be done. Martha had cleaning on her mind, Mary had Jesus on hers; Martha lost her temper, Mary listened in peace; Martha barked at the Lord, Mary worshiped him; Martha cried for help, Mary cried for more from the Master. Then Jesus said, "Martha, Martha. . . ." (Whenever my mom called my name twice in a row like that, the handwriting was on the wall. Like Chicken Little, I knew the sky would soon be falling.) He called her name twice and said, "Sit down for a change. You're wearing yourself out with your busy-work. Why, we're getting worn out ourselves just watching you! Would you prefer a tidy house or a tidy heart? Come listen for a while." (That's my original paraphrase of Luke 10:41–42).

Frustration aches to blame God. None of us enjoys topsy-turvy days. Smooth sailing gets our vote. Growth or no growth, give us the high road. The low road is for those who chill out on anxiety, fear, and pain. Silly us, to think we will never travel the low road. Even sillier to get mad at God when we do. It's like thinking that if God doesn't always pour sunshine on our parade, he is a bully, and we're not going to talk to him until he gives us back our peppermint. Blaming God is dumb. Praying makes a lot more sense. Catch Psalm 40, especially the first verse: "I waited patiently for the LORD; he turned to me and heard my cry."

With God, no mission is impossible. Not even bouncing back.

19 Vulnerability
Risky Business

While Jesus was in Bethany in the home of a man known as Simon the Leper, a woman came to him with an alabaster jar of very expensive perfume, which she poured on his head as he was reclining at the table (Matt. 26:6–7).

It is difficult to be open with people. They may reject you, or take advantage of you, or stab you in the back. A good friend of mine once said, after being rooked by a guy he thought was his friend, "Still, I have learned that it is worth it to take a thousand chances in reaching out. And, if all but one stab you in the back, you will have gained instead of lost." That's vulnerability.

Unless a Christian is willing to turn loose of his fears, defensiveness, and false fronts, he cannot be genuine and let people love him for who he is. Those who refuse to be vulnerable also unconsciously refuse to love and be loved. It's what C. S. Lewis described in *The Four Loves:*

> To love at all is to be vulnerable. Love anything, and your heart certainly will be wrung and possibly be broken. If you want to make sure of keeping it intact, you must give your heart to no one, not even to an animal. Wrap it carefully round with hobbies and little luxuries; avoid all entanglements; lock it up safely in the casket or coffin of your selfishness. But in that casket—safe, dark, motionless, airless—it will change. It will not be broken; it will become unbreakable, impenetrable, irredeemable. . . . The only place outside Heaven where you can be perfectly safe from all the dangers . . . of love is Hell.

Jesus was vulnerable. He allowed his disciples to see his true self. He didn't pretend to be one person on the outside while he was another on the inside. What's more, he let people get close to him. It was risky. As a matter of fact, it ended up costing his life. Judas, the betrayer, was the rotten ingrate who stabbed him in the back. But Jesus, even though he knew Judas's evil heart, let him get close anyway. That's vulnerability!

In our verse, Mary (John's Gospel mentions her name) comes with a pretty vase full of cologne—Ralph Lauren, Calvin Klein, or something expensive like that—and sprinkles it all over Jesus' head. The whole bottle! Obviously, this was a respected Jewish custom, because the Lord commended her for being so loving. Personally, I don't appreciate having anything dumped on my head. And I don't care much for perfume in my hair either. Who knows how big that vase may have been? Jesus probably was drenched in expensive cologne. John 12:3 says the whole house was filled with the fragrance. I would guess so! Just dump a bottle of sweet stuff on your cat and see if it doesn't smell up the whole house. Maybe even the whole neighborhood!

John 12:4–5 tells us another sidelight to the story. Judas, "the nonvulnerable one," was ticked off by Mary's open display of affection. She had broken her vase, something of value to her, and given away its contents for all to see. She was vulnerable. What she had sacrificed could never be retrieved. Would it be accepted or rejected? Judas disparaged her gift. The dollar signs rolled up in his eyes, and all he could think of was how stupid Mary was to waste rich perfume on Jesus. "It was worth a year's wages!" he screamed. I wonder what Mary's expression was when Judas criticized her act of love. I wonder if she cried.

Then Jesus went out on a limb to defend her:

"Leave her alone," said Jesus. "Why are you bothering her? She has done a beautiful thing to me. The poor you will always have with you, and you can help them any time you want. But you will not always have me. She did what she could. She poured perfume on my body beforehand to prepare for my burial. I tell you the truth, wherever the gospel is preached throughout the world, what she has done will also be told, in memory of her" (Mark 14:6–9).

What was the result of Jesus' willingness to share Mary's vulnerability? Judas popped his cork! That very night he went out and began to make arrangements to sell Jesus to his crucifiers (Mark 14:10–11). Isn't it interesting, though, that Judas himself was never really open. No one knew the real Judas. That was too bad for him, because he eventually couldn't stand himself any longer. Being all cooped up within himself, the old boy flipped out. He went over the edge and killed himself. What a terrible end to living a fraud. At last he was safe from all the dangers of love—in hell.

20 Rejection

The Sounds of Silence

"If the world hates you, keep in mind that it hated me first. If you belonged to the world, it would love you as its own. As it is, you do not belong to the world, but I have chosen you out of the world. That is why the world hates you" (John 15:18–19).

The apostles were a rejected band of misfits. God used them to touch thousands of lives, but they were hated by the world. They were so despised and rejected that every one of them suffered humiliating torture and death. According to tradition, here was their fate:

1. Matthew was martyred by being slain with a sword at a distant city of Ethiopia.
2. Mark died at Alexandria, after he was cruelly dragged through the streets of that city.
3. Luke was hanged on an olive tree in Greece.
4. John was boiled in a caldron of oil, but miraculously managed to escape and was later exiled to the distant island of Patmos, which means "my killing."
5. Peter was crucified at Rome, upside down.
6. James was shoved down from a peak of the temple, and what life was left in him was beaten out with a fuller's club.
7. Bartholomew was flayed like a fish, while he was alive.
8. Andrew preached to his persecutors from a cross until he died.
9. Thomas was run through with a lance at Coromandel, in the East Indies.
10. Jude was shot to death with arrows.
11. Matthias was stoned and then beheaded.
12. Paul, after various tortures and imprisonments, was beheaded in an elaborate ceremony before the Emperor Nero at Rome.

Surprised? You shouldn't be. Look again at Jesus' words in our title verse. The world hated and rejected the apostles because of their relationship with the Savior. You see, the most rejected human being ever to live was Jesus Christ. Listen to Isaiah's prophetic description of how he would be treated: "He was despised and rejected by men, a man of sorrows, and familiar with suffering. Like one from whom men hide their faces he was despised, and we esteemed him not. . . . But he was pierced for our transgressions, he was crushed for our iniquities . . ." (Isa. 53:3, 5).

John added a similar note to this sad song: "He came to that which was his own, but his own did not receive him" (John 1:11). I think he was talking about creation. In other words, we might translate John's words like this: "He came to his own creation, but those whom he had created would have nothing to do with him." And you know what? People—his creation!—are still rejecting him today.

Imagine how you would feel to be such an outcast from those you belong to or who belong to you. On a much smaller scale, consider your family. You're home from college for Christmas. Maybe the scene would go something like this, as you walk in the front door:

"Hi, Mom and Dad! It's good to be home." You smile and hug them, but they remain straight-faced and unresponsive.

"What are you doing here?" Your dad sounds distant.

"What do you mean? It's Christmas! Aren't you glad to see me?" You're a little hurt.

"Why didn't you just stay at college for Christmas?" Mom doesn't seem herself.

"Hey! Come on! Lighten up! Did I do something to upset you? Spend too much money, get bad grades or something?" You can't believe what's happening.

Your sistr comes into the room: "Oh, it's you. Did you *have* to come home?"

"What's the deal? Is this a joke or something? Come on, Sis, show me which presents are mine under the Christmas tree."

"There are no presents for you," your dad says seriously.

"No presents for me?" You're overwhelmed with confusion. "What on earth is wrong with you people! You act like you're on drugs. Are you all seeing a psychiatrist or something?"

Then your mom pulls something out of her purse. Offering it to you, she says, "I was afraid you might come home, so I went ahead and bought you this." You open it and find a bus ticket back to college.

Wouldn't that be a bizarre heartbreak? What ultimate rejection, to be snubbed by those closest to you. That's how it was for Jesus. He came to Bethlehem for Christmas but had to celebrate in the stable. And that, his first rejection, became the pattern for how he was treated throughout his life.

86

Now his words echo down the corridors of time (as the cliché goes) and tell us what to expect. If we follow Christ, we will not fit into this worldly society. As "normally" as we may live, our life in Jesus will separate us from those who want nothing to do with him. Furthermore, our clean lifestyle will be rejected by those accustomed to polluting their unbehaved hearts.

By the way, if you should decide to play the role of secret disciple—you know, an undercover Christian who acts like the world does to avoid being rejected—maybe you should meditate on the words of James: ". . . don't you know that friendship with the world is hatred toward God? Anyone who chooses to be a friend of the world becomes an enemy of God" (James 4:4). Bold talk, huh? So, you've got a choice: friendship with God, or friendship with the world. And, either way, rejection is a fact of life.

Let's just hope your family will welcome you home for Christmas.

21 | **Denial**

Playing Chicken

*Then he [Peter] began to call down curses on himself and he
swore to them, "I don't know the man!" Immediately a rooster
crowed. Then Peter remembered the word Jesus had spoken:
"Before the rooster crows, you will disown me three times."
And he went outside and wept bitterly (Matt. 26:74–75).*

Peter blew it. He did exactly what he swore he would never
do. He disowned the Lord and denied he ever knew him. But be
careful before you jump on the bandwagon and start downgrading
Peter. You, too, may be put in a situation where you will be tempted
to deny Jesus. A few examples? Okay.

You are at work and the crew is gathered around a fellow employee, razzing him about his faith in God. Will you walk away? Will you join in the verbal abuse? Will you come to the guy's defense? Jesus says, "I tell you the truth, whatever you did not do for one of the least of these, you did not do for me" (Matt. 25:45).

In class, one of your teachers is railing against the Bible and Christianity. Will you be silent? It is a form of denial if we do not do what Jesus said: "Neither do people light a lamp and put it under a bowl. Instead they put it on its stand, and it gives light to everyone in the house. In the same way, let your light shine before men, that they may see your good deeds and praise your Father in heaven" (Matt. 5:15–16).

At a family reunion, the conversation turns toward religion. You have a golden opportunity to share your faith with others. Will you do it? Or will you let the jam session roll on without letting your secret out of the bag? Matthew 10:32–33 holds an awesome truth worth pondering: "Whoever acknowledges me [Jesus] before men, I will also acknowledge him before my Father in heaven. But whoever disowns me before men, I will disown him before my Father in heaven."

Polycarp did not blow it. Is that a special hybrid of fish? No, Polycarp was the distinguished bishop of the church at Smyrna in the second century A.D. Eusebius recorded how the aged preacher—who was a link with the Apostolic Fathers and may have known John—took his stand against the Roman proconsul in the city stadium of Smyrna during some "games" at which several Christians had been martyred.

"Respect your years!" the proconsul shouted at the eighty-six-year-old Polycarp. "Swear by Caesar's fortune; change your attitude; say, 'Away with the godless!'"

The old man wouldn't budge. His jaws tightened, and he looked at the howling mob hungry for his blood. Waving his hand toward *them,* he looked up to heaven and cried out: "Away with the godless!" The crowd went wild with anger.

"Swear, and I will set you free: execrate Christ," the proconsul pressed him again.

Polycarp's answer has become famous in stories of the martyrs: "For eighty-six years I have been his servant, and he has never done me wrong: how can I blaspheme my king who saved me?"

"I have wild beasts," the proconsul threatened. "I shall throw you to them, if you don't change your attitude."

"Call them." The old geezer was fearless: "We cannot change our attitude if it means a change from better to worse. But it is a splendid thing to change from cruelty to justice."

"If you make light of the beasts," the governor smart-mouthed back, "I'll have you destroyed by fire, unless you change your attitude."

Again, Polycarp was as bold as a lion: "The fire you threaten burns for a time and is soon extinguished: there is a fire you know nothing about—the fire of the judgment to come and of eternal punishment, the fire reserved for the ungodly. But why do you hesitate? Do what you want."

The proconsul was berserk with rage and sent the crier to stand in the middle of the arena and announce three times: "Polycarp has confessed that he is a Christian." Then the frenzied mob screamed, "Burn him!" In moments the people rushed to place logs around the church elder and then stood quietly as he prayed: "O Father of thy beloved and blessed Son, Jesus Christ, through whom we have come to know thee, the God of angels, powers, and all creation, and of the whole family of the righteous who live in thy presence; I bless thee for counting me worthy of this day and hour, that in the number of the martyrs I may partake of Christ's cup, to the resurrection of eternal life of both soul and body in the imperishability that is the gift of the Holy Spirit."

Wow! What boldness! What a prayer! What bravery! At the sound of his "Amen!" the fire was lit and a great flame went shooting into the sky. Polycarp took his place in the Faith Hall of Fame—immortal forever!

Whether you or I will ever be faced with such a confrontation is uncertain. I hope I'm not. Although God gives grace to his children in times of persecution and martyrdom, I do not relish the idea of being tortured. However, by God's grace, I would never disown Jesus.

How weak we are to fear a little ridicule. Denial of Christ should never be an option. Peter denied him three times. But later, after righting this wrong, he went on to preach the gospel like a fireball. Until, one day, he was crucified hanging upside down.

Once you speak out for Christ, it gets easier. And, if you're tactful about it, people will respect you. But you know what? It feels good, deep down inside, to know you weren't afraid, that you really care enough about what you believe to say so. Something wells up inside, and the adrenaline flows. You think, "Hey! that wasn't so bad."

I'll bet you that's what Polycarp said when the fire carried him to heaven.

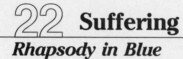 **Suffering**

Rhapsody in Blue

The men who were guarding Jesus began mocking and beating him. They blindfolded him and demanded, "Prophesy! Who hit you?" And they said many other insulting things to him (Luke 22:63–65).

A little boy, being asked what forgiveness is, gave this beautiful answer: "It is the odor that flowers breathe when they are trampled upon." Not bad for a kid, huh? Get the parallel? When Jesus was trampled upon, he emitted the aroma of forgiveness. Sometimes we must suffer for him in order that the world may catch a whiff of his presence. Those who accept suffering in stride are a fragrant reminder of the Savior's style when he walked among us.

Stephen, a disciple in the early church, followed the pattern perfectly. After a rousing sermon on hard-hearted resistance to Christ, the newly elected deacon was caught in a rock storm. The high priest led his buddies, the Pharisees, in a stoning contest to see who could kill the Jesus-freak first. What a way to react to a sermon! I've preached some bad messages in my life, but never bad enough that people tried to kill me. But Stephen's message was right on target. He had those religious fakes nailed to the wall.

As they were stoning him, Stephen began praying. His words echo the words of Christ when he was on the cross. Jesus said, "Father, forgive them for they do not know what they are doing." Compare Stephen's words, which he said while the rocks thudded against his body: "Lord, do not hold this sin against them" (Acts 7:60). As the flower was trampled, the smell of forgiveness was in the air.

While suffering is hardly a party experience, it can teach us valuable lessons. I remember a statement I read some time ago about God's sculpting process: "When God wants to do an impossible task, he takes an impossible individual and crushes him." God stamps the image of Christ on us by hammering and chiseling away the weak spots. He puts us through the fire and we come forth as gold.

Shadrach, Meshach, and Abednego learned this firsthand. They were stuck with a king named Nebuchadnezzar during the Babylonian captivity of Jerusalem. But they were tough as barbed wire. Old Nebbie wanted these three Israelite teenagers to worship the golden idol he had built in the plain of Dura. The false god was ninety feet high and nine feet wide. When the gutsy whipper-snappers wouldn't bow, he cooked up a nifty science experiment for them. They were going to observe how much heat the human body can withstand when thrown into a flaming furnace. Guess who the guinea pigs were? You got it. The third chapter of Daniel tells the story and gives us some hot tips on how to handle suffering:

Face the furnace. Regardless of the results, the fearless three were not going to buckle under pressure. "Furnace?" they said.

"Blazing furnace? Fine. Do what you're gonna do. But we won't worship your stupid image!" (another Earles paraphrase, of course). That isn't as easy as it sounds, because courage is not a cheap commodity. Especially when fire dancing is the penalty for having it.

There are different kinds of furnaces. Some are inflicted, and some are "typical," meaning they are a normal part of life. It is impossible to avoid some suffering in this existence. Which reminds me of an often-asked question: "If there is a God, why doesn't he do something about all of the suffering in the world?" Brilliant question. And what *should* he do? Create a utopia? He did that once, and human beings spoiled it. In choosing to sin, man brought upon himself certain consequences. Suffering is one of them. Now man blames God for letting suffering continue in the world. Talk about wanting your cake and eating it, too! Heaven's the only place void of suffering, because God is there and doesn't give humans the run of the place. Blaming God for not stopping suffering is like blaming your accountant because you can't pay your bills.

The message from the Hebrew kids is, "Face the furnace." And look for God in the fire, or else things will get mighty hot.

Meet him there. Just after becoming Nebbie's casserole, Shaddy, Meshy, and Abe had a partner join them in the flames. The king said that he looked like "a son of the gods." What do pagans know? Any simpleton can figure out who comforted them in the flames—Jesus! Who else? He is always present in our trials. He may not blow out the fire, but he doesn't make us go through it alone either. Because he knows what it means to suffer alone.

Great things follow. The sight of God's Son protecting the three teenagers was more than Nebuchadnezzar could handle. He called for them to come out of the furnace. And presto, they stepped out unharmed! Not one singed hair, not one minor blister, not even the smell of smoke. What a way to suffer! The king was so impressed by their faith and the miracle that he praised their God and forbade people to say anything against him. The guys got a promotion into the king's court. A happy ending. Except for one thing: they had still

94

experienced the furnace. Yes, they were courageous. And, yes, Jesus was with them. But still, they had to go into the flames. They had to be trampled upon. Then came the fragrance of their testimony. Such wonder baffles the world.

Ask Nebbie.

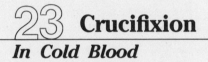 **Crucifixion**

In Cold Blood

And they crucified him. Dividing up his clothes, they cast lots to see what each would get (Mark 15:24).

Just try to comprehend the cross. Go ahead. Try. I've been collecting insights about what happened on Calvary for nearly twelve years, and the only thing I know for certain is that the more I learn about Jesus' gift, the more there is to learn—the more I understand, the more I realize how little I know. To some people the cross doesn't amount to much. In their minds, the crucifixion is just another one of history's sad stories. To others the cross is merely a religious status symbol—an ornament on the church steeple or a piece of jewelry to wear around the neck.

What difference does the cross make? What really happened on that day? Does it affect my life personally? Does it affect yours? Recently a pastor surveyed a hundred members of various churches about the significance of the cross. This is the question he asked: "Would it make any difference in your life if Christ had not died on the cross?" Remember now, he asked this question of *church members.* Here are the results:

45 said they didn't think it would make any difference.

25 said they thought so, but when asked what the difference would be, they weren't sure.

20 said it made all the difference in how they lived and believed.

10 said they didn't know, because they didn't understand what the cross was all about.

Can you believe that? Eighty out of a hundred church members didn't know the tremendous significance of the crucifixion and didn't understand how it is to affect our style of life. But stop. Hold everything! Which of those four groups are you in? Answer honestly. There are, no doubt, hundreds of people reading this who fit in with the eighty who are still in the dark about the greatest act of love of all time.

The crucifixion is the focal point of the gospel and the most important milestone in history. Those who refuse to stop, listen, and heed the signal of Calvary wreck their eternal souls, if not their earthly lives. You cannot ignore the cruel scene. Neither can you go away unaffected. To shut your ears only amplifies the sounds of Christ's agony; to turn your head away only magnifies the reality of why he was nailed there; to deny the awful event only clarifies the reason why he gave himself. Every time someone questions the importance of the cross, it's as if the Roman sledge is once again slamming into those spikes. The chilling, bone-crunching sound of metal against metal rings down through time.

Imagine being a centurion assigned to crucifixion detail on that day. It was a messy job. And I don't say that lightly. Deep down,

Roman guards must have hated the brutal duty of crucifixion. Prisoners screaming, fighting to escape, crying in agony, begging to die any other way. Several soldiers would be needed to hold down just one man. But not in Jesus' case; he lay down willingly.

First, the soldiers would extend the arms of their victim horizontally on the crossbar. Then they would drive wide spikes through either his hands or his wrists, and the blood would squirt onto the soldiers. Like an animal in the teeth of a steel trap, the poor guy would writhe and squirm to get free, only intensifying his pain by further ripping the flesh at his wounds. Meanwhile, the soldiers would lift the crossbar and put it into the socket of the vertical stake. Then, crossing one foot over the other, the feet were nailed in place, leaving enough bend in the knee to allow the crucified to pull himself up for a breath of air and prolong the agony. It was a grotesque job. And though most Romans appeared to relish their gory executions, there must have been times when the shrieks, and blood, and torture got to them. Maybe they were excited about killing Jesus, but it must have shook them that he died so willingly. So innocently.

Many strange things happened during the hours when Jesus hung in shame. So many that a book could be written about them alone. But in my limited understanding of Golgotha's tragedy, two things stand out to me:

1. Satan won, but he lost. The demons rejoiced on that infamous day. Jesus would no longer send them into a herd of pigs. Satan struck up the hard rock music of hell and the celebration began. "We finally got him, boys!" he screamed in his victory speech. "We've been after him for a long time, and today we nailed him and his goodie-goodie ideals to the rough-hewn tree. Final score: Satan wins, God loses." Right? Wrong!

Nice try, Dirt Face, but you lose. Although it was the wickedness of men that nailed him there, Jesus *chose* to die on the cross. He knew exactly what he was doing. Millions of soldiers could not have overpowered him had he not wanted to die. Legions of angels stood by and watched mysteriously, waiting for his summons. But God had

98

a master plan. A strategy to outsmart Satan. A counterpunch that became the knockout blow. When Jesus died, the cross became a bridge. Now men can come across it and escape Satan's pit. The Savior's death started a whole new age—an age in which God lives within his children and gives them life at its fullest.

Check it again. Final score: God conquers, Satan burns! Hear your fate, devil! He crushed your head; you scratched his foot, as Genesis 3:15 foretold.

2. *Jesus gave his life to give us life.* That's the gospel in a nutshell! The gospel is not about loving your fellow man. Nor is it about keeping the Ten Commandments. The "good news" is that Jesus offers us the same kind of life he lives—eternal! And it's made available to us via the cross.

Go there with me in the time travel of your mind's eye. See the Lord there. See your sins on him. See that you put him there. That I did. That we all did. See his life flow from him and admit that it should have been your own. See that he died as our Savior, and not as a martyr for a good cause. See that it was really sin that nailed him to the cross, and not Roman spikes. See that the sin was yours. Mine. Ours. Cry out for his forgiveness. Trust in him. Suddenly Golgotha is bathed in darkness. For a moment you can see nothing. Lightning strikes, and you see yourself on the cross. Then darkness. It strikes again and Jesus is in your place. Then darkness surrounds you again.

At last, when the clouds roll away, the cross is empty and laying on the ground. Jesus is standing nearby, smiling. And you hear him say: "Pick up your cross and follow me."

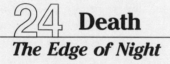 **Death**

The Edge of Night

> *When he had received the drink, Jesus said, "It is finished."*
> *With that, he bowed his head and gave up his spirit*
> *(John 19:30).*

I believe it was George Bernard Shaw who said, "The statistics on death are quite impressive: one out of every one people dies." That is impressive! And it's also in tune with what Scripture teaches: Man is destined to die (Heb. 9:27). My guess is, this chapter isn't among the first ones you flipped to. Death is not a very lively subject, if you get my drift. I mean, who wants to talk about rigor mortis, funeral music, and hearses? Especially when you're graduating. Right?

There are a couple of good reasons for digging into this topic. For

one, it bothers me that I pick up the newspaper every year at graduation time and read about students who were killed on the night of
their prom or commencement exercises because of wild, careless
partying. Mark it down: the Grim Reaper is not hesitant about taking
the young. If you go so crazy on graduation night that you lose
control of yourself, you may become another of death's impressive
statistics.

The second reason for doing a mini autopsy on this subject is to
face its reality. To get you thinking about life after death. To emphasize the importance of preparing to cross through the Valley of the
Shadow. Why skirt the issue? In my previous three commencement
journals for graduates, we looked under every rock and investigated
every dark crevice. Why do any differently now? Death is a fact of
life. So take a taste of reality straight from the pen of C. S. Lewis.
These words came from his heart. He wrote them shortly after the
death of his wife:

> Her absence is like the sky, spread over everything. . . . No one
> ever told me that grief felt so like fear. I am not afraid, but the
> sensation is like being afraid. The same fluttering in the stomach, the
> same restlessness, the yawning. I keep on swallowing.

Death has two fangs. There is a death of the spirit and a death of
the body. Paul alluded to this truth when he said, "For the wages of
sin is death, but the gift of God is eternal life in Christ Jesus our Lord"
(Rom. 6:23). On a similar note he wrote: "The sting of death is sin,
and the power of sin is the law. But thanks be to God! He gives us the
victory through our Lord Jesus Christ" (1 Cor. 15:56–57). So then,
there are two faces of death: physical and spiritual. Before we move
on (I know this stuff is thick and tough to chew), let me preempt this
dirge to bring you some "good news": God has provided eternal life
to fill the void of this dual death.

We can prepare for death by accepting God's gift of his Son. But in
some ways we can never really be ready to die. How can we? It's so

101

mysterious, and there's no one around who has experienced it to give us a rundown on what to expect. Death, I'm afraid, is one of those personal paths that we either walk alone or with Jesus. Basically, there are three ways to go, and two of them are bad. Scripture illustrates each with a true-to-life (or-death) example:

Example #1: Saul—The Violent Death. Saul was the first, once-glorious king of Israel. But he blew several opportunities to leave a lasting memory of righteousness for his people. Jealousy was his governor, and anger was the music of his soul. He lived by the sword, and he died by it, too. We are told in 1 Samuel 31:3 how he met his violent fate: "The fighting grew fierce around Saul, and when the archers overtook him, they wounded him critically." And a few verses later describe the gruesome aftermath: "The next day, when the Philistines came to strip the dead, they found Saul and his three sons fallen on Mount Gilboa. They cut off his head and stripped off his armor, and they sent messengers throughout the land of the Philistines to proclaim the news in the temple of their idols and among their people. They put his armor in the temple of the Ashtoreths and fastened his body to the wall of Beth Shan" (vv. 8–10). Without the head!

I've seen or heard about enough murder victims, gun-shot bodies, and drug-overdosed corpses to satisfy my curiosity. Believe me, more often than not, those who play in the fast lane die from reckless living. Ask John Belushi and John Lennon. This may sound tough, but it's true. What goes around comes around.

Example #2: Paul—The Tragic Death. The apostle was still young. He had a lot of mileage left in him. And yet he knew his days would be cut short by evil men. Read how this neon light of the gospel was turned out prematurely (humanly speaking): "For I am already being poured out like a drink offering, and the time has come for my departure" (2 Tim. 4:6). Paul was accepting the situation pretty well. But I can't help but wonder—what if he had lived another thirty years? Unexpected tragedies are so hard to take. "Why?" screams in our minds. No answer comes back. A car acci-

102

dent. A terrible fall. A rare disease. And, suddenly, what we never dreamed has become our worst nightmare.

Preachers are famous for funerals, and I've had my share of tragic ones. I remember comforting the mother of a six-year-old boy. His whole life was ahead of him as his mother watched him run across four lanes of traffic just before dark one night. Right before her eyes, a swift vehicle took him away from her. And no amount of comfort could ease the pain. I had no answers, only empathy and love. I hope I helped. I pray I did. That night I went home and held my kids and thanked God the tragedy wasn't mine.

Although I have no answers for sudden, unexplainable deaths, I do have one statement for you to roll over in your thoughts. Don't dismiss it. A ton of truth is buried within its words: From God's point of view there are no tragedies, because *he* makes no mistakes.

Example #3: Methuselah—The Natural Death. If it was ever time for anybody to die, it was time for Methuselah. He was 969 years old. Today, a hundred years is a ripe old age. But Meth brings new meaning to wrinkles. Of course, sin was not so rampant in the early years of mankind and had not yet decayed the health codes first created by God. So meet a man who lived to be a grandpa to the tenth-power.

All of us expect to live into the denture years to wear the gray-haired splendor of old age, as Proverbs 20:29 says. If this world lasts long enough, some of us will shrivel, and stoop, and gloat over great-grandchildren. Some of us, though, will go quickly, like a fast-flying comet in the night.

And the statistics on death will remain quite impressive.

 **Suicide**

Death Wish

So Judas threw the money into the temple and left. Then he went away and hanged himself (Matt. 27:5).

Another side of death. Hey! I know this is a downer subject, but the world has become a downer for thousands of people, and they are checking out by the droves! You may be on the verge of joining them. If not now, maybe someday. Let this chapter be etched in your memory. Come back to it anytime you need its ointment. Use it for yourself or a friend.

The epidemic of self-inflicted death is spreading so fast that sociologists can't keep up with the research to answer the "whys." Most counselors are treating symptoms instead of fighting germs, and as a result the hatch door to the back way out never gets locked. Here are the shocking facts:

Every minute a suicide is attempted in our country.

The suicide rate for Americans under the age of thirty has increased 300 percent in the past ten years.

Women attempt suicide four times as often, but men are three times more successful.

Eighty percent of suicide victims have tried it previously.

Approximately three suicides occur every hour. That's over seventy per day. Day in—day out. Week in—week out. All year long.

Suicide is the ninth-leading cause of death in older adults, the third-leading cause of death in young adults, and the second-leading cause of death in teenagers.

In America—land of the free and home of the brave—there are 24 percent more deaths by suicide than by murder.

The latest statistics reveal an acute increase in suicides among young black women.

My brushes with those on life's tightrope have been increasingly more frequent. The methods are usually grisly: poison, pills, guns, asphyxiation, jumping from a bridge or a building, electrocution, razor blades, or an intentional car wreck. Sometimes the attempt fails, and the survivor and his or her family must live with the consequences: severe brain damage, a "vegetable" existence, expensive skilled care in a nursing home, and permanent scars on all pleasant memories. The grief comes in waves, subsiding only to be replaced by new waves of shock, which are replaced by a range of emotions no one comprehends except those who have been there.

Prepare yourself for what's coming up. If you've got a weak stomach, get hold of yourself. It is not my intention to be sensational or disgusting, but I want to unload some facts about suicide rarely

105

considered. They are ugly facts, but sometimes reality is ugly. Maybe it will be ugly enough to turn some people away from suicide's selfish grip of self-pity. Consider this:

Who finds the corpse? Usually a family member. And the scene is never pretty. What mother deserves to find her son with his wrists slit open, lying in pools of blood? What dad deserves to find his daughter with her eyes rolled up in her head, blackened tongue hanging out from an intentional overdose of pills? Think! Would you want your brother to find you with half your head shot off? Do you want your friends to have to come to the morgue and identify your mangled body because you decided to end it all by going over an embankment? Make up your mind now—while you're under control—not to meditate on suicide as an option in solving your problems.

Who cleans up the mess? You may not like the thought of this, but it's one of the untold nightmares of suicide. Somebody has to wash the blood and brains off the wall. Sickening? That's suicide. That's what the selfish voice that says "Pull the trigger" never tells you. Somebody has to drag the body out of the garage and flush the stench of death from the house. Somebody has to clean up the vomit, or scrape up whatever's left of the body. It's vile. It's gross. You might think it shouldn't be mentioned. But I do. Suicide may seem easy, even glamorous, but the mess it leaves behind can never be washed from the minds of those who see it.

Who pays for it? I mean, who suffers? Parents who torture themselves for all the ways they went wrong. A spouse who feels the ultimate pain of failure but has no way of asking forgiveness or making changes. A brother or sister who wishes family ties had been a little closer. A friend who fights surging feelings of inadequacy and helplessness. Who pays? The people who live on, that's who. And why? Because, in the clutches of deep self-pity, no other answer comes through, and some miserable soul leaps into eternity.

I'm often asked: "Do you think a person can commit suicide and still go to heaven?" In other words: "Can someone kill himself and

106

still be considered a Christian?" Admittedly, it is hard to imagine a believer copping out on life. Suicide is the highest form of unbelief. It means not even God can be trusted to help. However, only God knows a person's true spiritual condition. It is not for us to say whether or not a self-killer goes to heaven.

Something to think about, though: Hebrews 10:31 says, "It is a dreadful thing to fall into the hands of a living God." Suicide does not seem like a wise way to suddenly meet the Creator.

Do not forget these words. Earmark the pages if you have to. You may need to read them again someday. By the way, ten people attempted suicide while you read this chapter. One was successful.

 **Grief**

Silent Screams

Jesus wept (John 11:35).

I wanted to write this chapter yesterday, but my whole day got fouled up. Today I know why. God wanted me to see grief close up before I wrote about it. One of my good friends came into my office a few minutes ago, seeking comfort. His mother had just died. I cried with him. It was no time for pretty platitudes. Or drumming up old memories. Or reading Scripture. Or repeating God's promises of eternal life for his saints. It was a time when only crying would do. Then we ached out a prayer.

Grief: traumatic state of emotional shock. This monster is generally associated with the pain we feel at the loss of a loved one.

However, that is not the only time we feel its steely clutches. The same emotions of grief creep in when . . .

A love relationship is fractured and thrown overboard.

A long-awaited dream is shattered and becomes impossible.

You are greeted at the office Christmas party with a pink slip. Hello, unemployment!

Your company suddenly relocates you in the boondocks away from relatives and friends.

Through tragic circumstances, you lose an eye or use of a limb.

Your house burns down.

The family pet gets run over by a car.

You find out that you do not get to graduate because you flunked one course.

Although grief is painful, it is a natural part of the healing process. And any range of reactions may be a part of the mending: sobbing, screaming, blank silence, hostility, trembling, fainting, hyperactivity, tantrums, or withdrawal. None of these should last too long. But they are necessary to venting grief. Otherwise, our cooped-up emotions will implode into depression. "You mean 'explode,' don't you?" you're wondering. No. I mean *implode*. That's an internal explosion, a bursting inward. It blows up your emotions. The big hole it leaves inside of you is called depression.

Welcoming grief is difficult to do. And yet, just as a cast is essential in mending a broken leg, grief is crucial to recovery from heartache. "Yeah, but how do I recover from grief?" you may be thinking. Well, not by listening to the shallow shibboleths doled out by the most dutiful Christians. You have heard them, haven't you?

"This must be God's will, so just accept it!"

"Death is only the beginning, and your loved one is in a better place now."

"Just dwell on the good things you have left in life."

"You still have the rest of your family to love and care for."

"If you think your situation is bad, consider what others have gone through."

One thing you can do is turn to Jesus Christ. Isaiah 53:3 tells us that he was "a man of sorrows, and familiar with suffering." And the lead verse of this chapter records his grief at the death of one of his good friends, Lazarus. Jesus does understand. And while you may not feel like talking to him at first (he understands that, too!), he's ready when you are. Besides, opening up to him is better than condemning yourself with such negative grief talk as "If only I had. . . ."

Another prescription that can speed the healing is being able to recognize the different stages of grief. At least it will help you to understand what you're going through. There are five of them:

Stage One: Denial. During this stage, individuals refuse to believe what is happening to them. I remember ministering at the funeral of a child and hurting as the mother demanded to have the casket opened to verify that her little one was in there. She had already looked three times. After the casket was closed for the final time, she said that it didn't look like her child and maybe he was at home waiting for her. I put my arm around her and said, "No. We must go to the graveside." Denial is a normal reaction, but unless it is only momentary, recovery will be slow in coming. If it comes at all.

Stage Two: Anger. This almost always includes anger toward God for not stopping the loss from occurring. Frequently I have been asked, "Well, if God is God, then why didn't he do something?" Usually my response is the same: "I can't answer for God." People don't want theological answers at times like these.

Stage Three: Guilt. Some grief-guilt is false. By that I mean that people just harass themselves with "What I should have done's." At

110

other times the guilt is valid. A rebellious son is too late to say "I'm sorry"; a careless husband wishes he had been more attentive; a friend knows the friendship was severed because of something he did (or didn't) do. By the way, this is the snag stage. People get hung up here the longest. And it can cause deep depression.

Stage Four: Real Grief. Initially there is shock. Then the first wave of grief. Then come stages one, two, and three. Real grief occurs weeks after the loss. After everybody goes home. After reality sets in. After life begins to go on. After the memories become pleasant again. This is when the tears of healing take place.

Stage Five: Resolution. Once the first four stages run their course, this stage is almost automatic. Joy gradually returns, and the bereaved sees that life is still worth living.

Amy Carmichael, the famous missionary to India and devotional writer, once commented on how grief leads us to experience the deepest inner changes. She said: "The eternal essence of a thing is not in the thing itself but in one's reaction to it. The distressing situation will pass, but one's reaction toward it will leave a moral and spiritual deposit in his character which is eternal."

Chew on that. And watch out for implosions.

 **Resurrection**

No Stone Unturned

Then he went up and touched the coffin, and those carrying it stood still. He said, "Young man, I say to you, get up!" The dead man sat up and began to talk, and Jesus gave him back to his mother (Luke 7:14–15).

No one ever died in Jesus' presence. At least we have no record of it. And some who were already dead, he called back to life. A funeral could become a celebration when Jesus was around. Deaths became resurrections. Grief became astonishment. Miseries were transformed into miracles. Sadness reversed into smiles. And tragic endings became sudden, fresh beginnings.

His own resurrection was no small wonder. He predicted it ahead of time, which increased the impact of its effect when the stone was

112

rolled away from death's door exactly as he promised it would be. Whether he was injecting new life into those who were given up for dead or stepping out of the grave himself, Jesus left no stone unturned.

The resurrection of Jesus Christ is a major part of the gospel. For if Jesus could conquer our sins by dying for them but could not triumph over death itself, then neither could we force death to wave the white flag of surrender. We cannot live forever unless he can live forever—unless there is life after death for him. What David did to Goliath, Jesus had to do to death. And he did!

Imagine the villainous conversation that may have taken place between Satan and Dr. Death as Jesus was laid to rest. They would have conspired to hold him. Every day the Evil One checked to be sure that Death's iron shackles were still in place. Hear him as he dropped by on the first day.

"Oh, Death, do you have him? Is he locked up tight? Does he show any signs of coming back to life?"

"Do not fret yourself, Apollyon! The man they called King of the Jews is safe in my grasp. You surely do not think I would break our bargain and let him go!" Dr. Death answered.

"Good! Good!" Satan shouted as he stalked into the cosmos. And then a burst of shrill laughter pierced the thick dungeon of hell.

Still, his fear urged him to double-check on day two. "Is all well, Death, ol' boy? Does the prince continue to rest in peace? Has he moved or shown any sign of life?"

"You doubt my power to hold him!" Death's reply was fueled with rage. "Peek at him then, if you must. Does he look dead enough to you?" Satan was quite pleased to have the chance to see the Son of God stiff and lifeless.

"He looks quite dead."

"I assure you, he is."

With that, the foe of righteousness went upon his way. But in the back of his mind lingered the vague memory of Jesus' words— something about the third day. Right away the eternal scumball decided to visit again tomorrow. Fear panicked its way through his thoughts until he was inside the tomb again. What a comfort it was to see Dr. Death gripping the carpenter from Nazareth with such a sure hold.

"Back again, Abaddon?"

"Yes, this one worries me."

"Why? He's just a man. And no man yet has broken my strong cords unless God himself turned the key in the locks."

"That's what scares me. Do you know what it will mean if he rises again! He will become the Savior of mankind."

"You're a worry-wart! I've got him. Can't you see? Why don't you go about your business of tormenting people and leave me alone. If he hasn't come alive by now, he isn't going to."

Just then a quake shook the spot. "What was that?" the devil whispered like a coward. Then the whole tomb began to tremble like the lone leaf left on a tree in late autumn.

"Something is wrong." Even Death sounded afraid. "I can feel him moving. He's trying to get loose of me!"

"Well, hold him, you stupid fool!"

"I'm trying to! I . . . I'm . . . I'm . . . losing . . . him. Oh, no! He's crushing me! And he has taken the keys away from me." Then, in a flash, Dr. Death died. Satan hit his hyper-space button. And Jesus reclaimed his crown as the Prince of Life. Motioning to the entrance of the tomb, Christ did what Buddha and Mohammed will never do: he rolled away death's door and brought himself to life.

Today, his inspiring words pour zest into our hearts: ". . . Because I live, you also will live" (John 14:19). Goliath loses again.

114

28 Doubt

The Fear of Believing

*When the other disciples told him [Thomas] that they had
seen the Lord, he declared, "Unless I see the nail marks in his
hands and put my finger where the nails were, and put my
hand into his side, I will not believe it" (John 20:25).*

In his popular book *Come Before Winter,* Charles Swindoll
relates an event from the life of Erich Weiss, the highest-paid enter-
tainer at the turn of this century. On March 10, 1904, the *London
Daily Illustrated Mirror* designed a pair of handcuffs especially for
the famous escapologist. Weiss accepted their challenge. And get
this: each cuff had six locks and each lock had nine tumblers. A
crowd of four thousand antsy spectators came to witness the dem-
onstration one week later at the Hippodrome.

Weiss knelt down out of sight into an empty case that came waist-high. Twenty minutes later he stood up, setting off a round of cheers. But he was still handcuffed. He went down again, this time for fifteen minutes. More applause erupted, but Weiss was still in the locks. Twenty minutes later he stood up and jumped out of the cabinet. The crowd went wild. But he still wasn't free.

Flexing his hands carefully, the master magician reached inside his vest and took out a small pocketknife. He opened the knife with his teeth and put the handle in his mouth. Then he bent over, allowing his long coattails to fall over his head. In moments he had cut the coat to pieces to escape its binding restrictions. The crowd howled with excitement as Weiss hopped back into the box. Down he went again. The crowd murmured while the magician labored out of sight. Ten minutes later the escape was complete. With the handcuffs held above his head, Weiss climbed out of the cabinet. The audience flipped out.

The magician later explained that he could have freed himself right away, but he wanted to give the crowd a show. Then he emphasized what he said before in many interviews: "My brain is the key that sets me free!" Erich Weiss is remembered as the greatest escape artist of all time. Don't recognize the name? Maybe you know him better as Harry Houdini.

Did you catch what Houdini claimed was the key that opened the locks? *His brain.* Houdini had faith in his ability. He believed in himself. He didn't know how to doubt. No challenge was too big for him. The result? Houdini accomplished more incredible feats in his lifetime than any other performer, and today his work is considered to be the benchmark for magicians.

Thomas was not such an optimist. After the resurrection he was the hardest one to convince that Jesus was alive. But why? I'm sure Doubting Tom wanted to believe. He had been among the disciples throughout the teaching ministry of Christ. Jesus had spelled out the third-day concept to them all. It should have at least rung a bell

116

with Tom. Whether it did or not, he refused to believe what he could not see.

The world is well stocked with people like Tom. Their problem? Fear of believing. Tom was afraid to believe because he was afraid to be wrong. If he had believed and turned out to be wrong, his whole world would have caved in. Thousands can relate to that. They dream dreams as big as life, but they're afraid to attempt them. Just because they fear failing. Sometimes they fear success. Know any people like this?

An entire week passed after Thomas refused to believe. I wonder what those seven days were like for him. No doubt he was certain that Jesus was dead for good. All of the chatter about the resurrection must have seemed like meaningless drivel to him. Tom had dared Jesus to prove himself, but for seven days it was a no-show. It sort of reminds me of the way some people refuse to trust in Jesus Christ until he sends a sign especially for them. Foolishness!

Faith doesn't have a neutral gear. People who truly believe are on the move. Maybe that's why some people are afraid to believe in anything. They know it may cost them energy and effort. It was easy for Tom to say, "I'll believe it when I see it!" That required nothing but a soft chair to sit on.

As you set sail for your destiny, faith will be your rudder. Faith in God and faith in his Word. Faith in yourself and in God's eagerness to bless you. Without faith you will become a shipwreck. Or, at the very best, you will drift aimlessly.

But don't let me forget: Jesus did put in an appearance for Thomas. What a shame that the doubter could never say, "I believed it was true before I saw it, because you promised you'd be back."

Had Erich Weiss feared to believe, he never would have become the great Houdini. And, if Jesus had not cured Thomas's doubting, the play-the-percentages disciple would have been bound with spiritual handcuffs that not even Houdini could escape.

29 **Apocalypse**

A Space Odyssey

"But in those days, following that distress, 'the sun will be darkened, and the moon will not give its light; the stars will fall from the sky, and the heavenly bodies will be shaken'" *(Mark 13:24–25).*

As our family was traveling through beautiful Snowmass Village, sister city of Aspen, Colorado, a huge clump of cumulus clouds were hovering above majestic Snowmass Mountain. The sun was behind the cloud bank, and its rays were streaming from around the edges, presenting a pretty picture to start off our vacation on the right foot. Instantly I was struck with the glory of the scene, and my imagination began to envision what the end of this age will be like. If angels had fired up with the "Hallelujah Chorus," I wouldn't have been surprised.

It seemed like a perfect time to give a visual lesson to my kids. "Look at the sun shining around that cloud!" I glanced at Jared and Sara in my rearview mirror. "Just think," I spoke dramatically as they leaned over the front seat, "one of these days Jesus is going to come back to this earth riding on a cloud. It probably will look a lot like that one."

Sara is still young enough to be easily impressed. She responded excitedly, "Yeah, and that's gonna be so pretty!"

Silence fell over us as we continued up the mountain drive to the condominium where we were staying. The kids settled back in their seats, and we continued to drink in the view. Then, out of nowhere, Jared spoke his concern.

"Dad?"

"Yes."

"I hope Jesus waits until after our vacation."

What a mouthful! Jared speaks for the multitudes, doesn't he? How many times have people said, "I hope Jesus won't come until . . ."? The wish list that would delay Christ's return might get quite long. Here's a sampling. I've heard all of these fill-in-the-blank wishes to the statement "I hope Jesus doesn't come until after . . ."

. . . we get married and have sex.

. . . our first grandchild is born.

. . . Christmas.

. . . our baby is born.

. . . my parents are saved.

. . . I graduate.

. . . we move into our new home.

. . . my first semester of college.

. . . the concert this weekend.

. . . my children are saved.

Being human, it's natural for us to anticipate life's milestones. We can't help but look forward to the special times—as few as there actually are on this planet—and hope we don't miss any of them. But it reveals a weak spot in our understanding of the great hereafter. God won't shortchange us. We won't be blessed with less in heaven than we have here on earth. Of course, it is another dimension. Still, we must be careful not to sink our roots too deeply in this world.

Balance is the key. How about some "do's and don'ts"? I know how much you love them.

Do watch for him. Jesus finished his description of the greatest space odyssey man will ever witness by saying, "What I say to you, I say to everyone: 'Watch!'" (Mark 13:37). In other words, be heads-up. Keep his return in your thoughts and let your imagination run when the clouds roll in.

Don't set dates. Last year there were a half-dozen predictions about which day Jesus would sweep down to end it all. Each one passed with no fireworks and no apocalypse. Jesus was plain on this point: "You also must be ready, because the Son of Man will come at an hour when you do not expect him" (Luke 12:40). Please permit me to yell one thing at the top of my lungs: "Don't listen to the lunatics and dimwits who use homemade mathematics to calculate the day of his arrival!" Okay. I'm finished. Thank you.

Do keep shaking. Watching for Christ doesn't mean you have to sell everything and move into a commune in the mountains. It doesn't mean you jam your head into the sand and ignore the world around you. Christians still have the responsibility of sprinkling out of the saltshaker into the world.

Don't go on a binge. Nothing bores me like a Christian who loses his mind over "last things." These types attend every prophecy seminar. They own every book on the great tribulation and the

120

second coming of Christ. The only sermons they care about are the ones on Christ's return. And their favorite book of the Bible? Revelation, of course. Watch? Yes. Be ready? Yes. Tell others he's coming? Yes. Freak out on the subject? No—don't push it too far.

Right, Jared?

3⃝ Timing
Grasping the Moment

"Dear woman, why do you involve me?" Jesus replied, "My time has not yet come" (John 2:4).

Charles Cowan, missionary to the Orient, wrote these words to a friend: "Be spiritually alert. God keep us from duties evaded, capacities wasted, opportunities neglected, the God-given life slipping away from our grasp."

He sounds very much like Paul when the motivated apostle wrote: "Be very careful, then, how you live—not as unwise but as wise, making the most of every opportunity, because the days are evil" (Eph. 5:15–16). Paul wrote his Epistle to the Ephesians from Rome. A few years after the letter was mailed, Rome was burned and the Christians were blamed. It wasn't long before Paul died a martyr's death at the hands of Nero. The apostle had not squandered his time. He made the most of every opportunity and grasped all that God wanted him to finish.

Not everyone is so organized. Take, for instance, the businessman who had these letters in a large frame on his wall: PITTOT. They stood for "Procrastination is the thief of time." Those who procrastinate always miss God's timing. And, as a result, they miss God-given opportunities. Lost opportunities are often the difference between failure and success. An old rhyme has it right:

> Procrastination, thief of time,
> Monster in my breast;
> You would steal God's gift sublime;
> And rob me of heaven's best.

What if Paul had been off on his timing? A half-dozen churches wouldn't have been started; most of the New Testament wouldn't have been written; thousands of people wouldn't have heard the gospel; Silas would have traveled alone; and Timothy would have ended up in some liberal seminary. Can you imagine how Paul might have responded to the church at Antioch when they wrote for him to come? (Antioch was where he got his start.) Had he missed that opportunity, his whole life would have been altered. If Paul had been a man unaware of God's timing, he might have written back something like this:

Dear Friends in Antioch:

I can't believe how swamped business is here in Tarsus. Tentmaking is such a tedious job, and I'm already three months behind. If things keep going like they are, the Christmas rush will kill me. Besides that, the paperwork is spread out all over my desk. I probably need an accountant, but there's no time to interview one. Concerning your invitation to minister, I can't come on Friday because Tarsus is playing Rome in the Super

Bowl, and I have tickets in the front row. How about next
month?

Signed,

Paul

P. S. Why don't you send Barnabas up for a visit? He can go to
the big game with me.

Absurd? Yes. But many Americans schedule their lives like that.
They are too busy to do the really important things, but they can
always find time for entertainment. Naturally they pay the piper a
fine price, since they are never ready for what God has prepared for
them. Like the bulky football player who can't get the timing of the
quarterback's cadence, they are always offside.

There are four types of timing. As you continue to mature in your
use of time you will experience each one of them.

Wrong time . . . wrong place. Some of you may feel like this is
the story of your life. Totally out of sync. You're never where you
want to be, never where you ought to be. You usually find yourself
saying or doing the wrong things. Your ideas are either way before
their time or just catching up with last year's fad. Being in the wrong
place at the wrong time can be painful. Ask Goliath.

Wrong time . . . right place. It is possible to be exactly where
God wants you but not be doing what God wants you to do. John
Mark is an example of being in the right place at the wrong time. A
comparison of Acts 13:13 and 15:37–38 reveals that the freshman to
the ministry was traveling with the troupe of Paul and Barnabas.
Great place to be. But young John Mark went home early. He had a
serious case of bad timing.

Right time . . . wrong place. This may be the saddest combina-
tion of jumbled timing. In Judges 16:25–30, Scripture details the
mighty power of Samson. The heathen Philistines were paying
homage to their god, Dagon, when Samson shoved the pillars of the
temple down and the building filled with people was crushed. An

124

event that Rambo would have respected. One problem: Samson should not have been in Philistia. Few things in life are as disheartening as accomplishing great things in the wrong place. It cost Samson his life.

Right time . . . right place. That's Jesus Christ. He was never out of step, never out of sync. Every time the clock ticked during his thirty-three years, Jesus was precisely where he was supposed to be. When he cried, "It is finished!" at his death, not a single task had been left undone. He was always in haste, but never in a hurry. Jesus was the master of right timing.

And he didn't need a PITTOT sign to remind him.

Focus

20/20 Vision

He looked up and said, "I see people; they look like trees walking around" (Mark 8:24).

Here is a puzzling little episode. Jesus has come to visit the town of Bethsaida. As usual, a crowd gathers and a blind man waits hopefully. Several people are begging Jesus to heal the man, but he doesn't like their pushy, gimme attitude. Figuring that they probably cared to see an incredible act of power more than they really sympathized with the poor fellow, the Lord took him outside of town for a secret session.

Once they were away from the hubbub of the needy multitudes, Jesus pulled the man close and spit on his eyes. What a bizarre method of healing! Try that at a hospital sometime and see how it goes over. Just walk into some guy's room and tell him that you have the remedy for his malady. Then bend over and spit on him. See if that doesn't stir him up. Tell him Jesus did it that way. Go ahead. Know what will happen? The boys in the white jackets will haul you away to a room with padded walls. Just the same, Jesus used spit-healing on the blind man.

Seriously, it wasn't the spit that gave the man eyesight. Faith did it. Faith always does it. But look again at the passage in Mark 8. The man didn't get his vision back immediately. In the distance he could see people, but they were sort of fuzzy. They had the appearance of tree limbs flapping in the breeze. Question: Why wasn't he healed immediately like all the rest? Maybe he had a problem with his focus button. Don't laugh. I'm referring to the focus of his faith. Maybe Jesus only spit to test the man's faith. He found that the man wanted to believe but may have been concentrating harder on seeing than believing.

Jesus touched him again. I like that. Aren't you glad for second chances? What if lightning zapped us on first mistakes? Not only would we have zero population growth, but the babies would be left to take care of themselves. Worse than nuclear fallout! But it isn't that way. God is the God of the second chance. On the second touch the man regained his sight. Jesus didn't give up on him. Where would you be if Jesus gave up on you?

The blind man's story suddenly sparkles with significance, huh? Cast your eyes upon three other lessons that at first glance seem like blurry trees:

1. There are two kinds of blindness. You got it—spiritual and physical. The double touch illustrates man's need to be cured of spiritual blindness in order to have true 20/20 vision. For even though you may see every blessed color of creation, if you can't focus on the Creator through eyes of faith, then you're blinder than the blind. The result of the first touch is an ideal symbol of physical eyesight. The man could see but he couldn't. If you get my drift. The second touch really opened his eyes. Whoosh! Add three-dimensional focus and the meaning of life becomes as easy to spot as white lint on black velvet.

2. *The man was nearsighted.* Obviously, right? Go a step farther. Was the man more preoccupied with just being able to see than he was with seeing what really counted? It's hard to say. Anybody would have been excited to see for the first time. Maybe Jesus was trying to make a point. Not only to teach the man, but us, too. If so, then what is it? Just this: If we zoom in too much on our own little world, then everything around us will gradually turn into one fat blur. The gospel has high-powered lenses. Its users become farsighted. They are people of vision.

3. *Sight is a miracle.* Not just eyesight. Although it is glorious to have the privilege of seeing life's splendors: snow crocus in late winter . . . a colt climbing to his legs for the first time . . . majestic mountains rising above a carefully planted valley . . . babies . . . maple trees in the fall . . . good movies . . . the face of a familiar friend . . . waterfalls . . . puppies licking a tickled child . . . plus a million more. And yet, the one who sees all of that but still focuses on the bigger picture, that's the one who knows the full miracle of sight. Seeing details is a small miracle compared to being able to see life itself.

And to think that so much truth could come from one wad of spittle.

Before I finish this book and you begin to conquer the world, permit me to share my favorite verse in the Gospels. John records it at the close of his account of Jesus' life: "Jesus did many other things as well. If every one of them were written down, I suppose that even the whole world would not have room for the books that would be written" (John 21:25). That in itself speaks volumes.

Step into a dark world—and have a shining life!